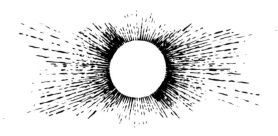

RADICAL ENLIGHTENMENT

My Guy On The 9th Floor

To Jackie,

Take what you need, leave what you don't

Much love,

Kevin Russell

A Handbook For Leveling-up Your Consciousness,
Fulfillment, and Connection To Your Higher Self

Kevin Russell

ISBN: 978-1-7353492-0-6 (paperback)
ISBN: 978-1-7353492-1-3 (ebook)
ISBN: 978-1-7353492-2-0 (audiobook)

Printed in the United States of America
First Printing - August, 2020

Editing: Talyor Graham (rabbitandleo.com) & Matti Sand (mattisand.com)
Illustrations & Diagrams: Kevin Russell *(unless otherwise noted)*
Cover Design: Camron Clark (camronclark.com)
Interior Design: Kevin Russell

Published by Radical Enlightenment, LLC
radicalenlightenment.com

Acknowledgments

A very special thank you
to my parents, Kelli Russell, Ryan Russell, Jenny Harkleroad, Dr. Warren Jacobs, Julz Smith, Jarmal Beavers, Carla Cole, Michael Stubblefield, and Larry Kessler for their impact on my personal journey at all the right times.

Thank you also to all the philosophers, writers, scientists, thinkers, and doers throughout time, and all the open minds and dreamers of the world for fostering the expansion of our human experience.

Contents

Section IV - Priming the System: Becoming the Observer of Your Own Fourth-Dimension

Section I

_____

The First Part

"*One does not become enlightened by
imagining figures of light,
but by making the dark conscious.*"

– Carl Jung

Today

 I woke up late again today,
and rushed to eat breakfast in the car.

I drove too fast again today,
Praying to get that last parking spot.

School dragged on again today.

Same classes, same people,
same mindless curriculum, same teenage bullshit.

I got home early from school today,
and bummed a ride to the beach.

But the beach was closed today.

Someone decided to park their boat neatly on the reef,
and it hemorrhaged oil and gas, leaching its toxicity into the world.

My mom was gone again today,
when I finally got back home.

I took a shower for a long time today,
letting the warm building blocks of life cascade
off my body and tumble down the drain.

Standing naked in my darkened room,
dripping wet from a sadness I couldn't explain,

I put the cold barrel of a gun in my mouth today.
But I didn't pull the trigger, not yet,

Not today.

- Me (eighteen years old)

Prologue

Life isn't always easy.

Regardless of what language or culture we are born into, we all emerge into a world foreign to us. When we are little, most likely the only tools we are given to navigate life, for better or for worse, are the ones our parents give us . . . if we are lucky. Most likely, the tools they give *us* are the ones *they* were given by their parents, and our grandparents got their tools from their parents, and so on and so on.

Growing up, navigating adolescence, going through puberty, traversing social scenes, performing in school, figuring out who we are, entering and navigating "adult life" can get really overwhelming.

I wrote the poem on the previous page in writing seminar during my senior year of high school. I was eighteen at the time and bound for college, working three or four nights a week, doing well in school, looking forward to being out on my own in just under a year's time, and I didn't think I was depressed or distressed about anything particular. Probably (okay, *definitely*) some "teenage angst" every now and then. But at some point that fall, the thought had popped into my head: *"What if I wasn't here anymore? What if I committed suicide?"*

The thought confused me, and it frightened me. *"Where did that come from? Why would I even think that?"*

However, instead of pushing it down, or ignoring it and hoping it would go away, or running away from it or letting it fester, I turned to face it. It was almost a challenge to myself. And I pitted the voice in my head against, well, me.

"Okay, you're the one who had this thought, so let's go there, tough guy. Take it all the way. Put yourself in that situation, put yourself in that mentality. Feel what it would be like to be in that place, and what it would feel like to take that action. Now think about someone besides yourself. If you decide to leave this life, you destroy other lives besides your own. See your mom, sister, and dad after you do it. Your friends. Imagine what it will feel like for them after you're gone."

And I did. I let myself go there in my mind. I followed it all the way past the hypothetical suicide to the impact that action would have on those that remained. I let myself feel the anguish, hurt, anger, sadness, frustration, hopelessness, loneliness, desperation, confusion, and pain that must come with thoughts of taking your own life, and that those left behind must feel as well. I let myself feel all of these things and as I did, I confirmed this was absolutely not the path for me.

Then I let all the feelings go, as well as the original thought that had popped into my head. I released every bit of the thought experience, and I made sure that nothing was left behind.

This was the first time I can remember giving myself the space to sit with a challenging thought and follow the trail of that thought further than I had ever been willing to go before.

It was challenging and emotional, and scary, but the moment after I let everything around the experience go, my internal perspective shifted. It felt like it had expanded *ever-so-subtly* and I had a little more internal space than a few minutes prior.

I had no way of knowing it at the time, but this was the beginning of what would become my journey to meet My Guy on the 9th Floor.

Introduction

I was forty-one years old when I first met "My Guy." He's always positive, always encouraging, pretty hilarious, crazy smart, and beyond insightful. In my mind, he looks like me because he *is* me, or my higher self, anyway. My soulful self, higher consciousness, inner-god—whatever label you ascribe to the 'highest-good-that-is-also-you'—that is whom I met.

Connecting with him was like meeting myself again, but for the first time. It felt more like a home than any house I'd ever lived in. For me, it was a surge of blindingly positive energy that erupted through my body, starting at my heart, blooming through my torso, and finishing in my head. I felt the electricity of it in every sinew and every cell. It was explosive and electric and accompanied by a profound flash of brilliant white light that I felt and saw *internally*. An overwhelming sense of peace, inspiration, joy, abundance, and love washed over me and cascaded through me, like an avalanche racing down a mountain. He was me and I was him, slightly apart but vibrantly connected at the same time. It was like the voice in my head was suddenly somehow a little different, changed for the better. I heard, with a surge of overwhelmingly positive emotion, "*Yes!* I am so glad you made it. We are going to have so much fun together."

This book is the culmination of our first bit of "fun." These words and ideas catalyzed in me and were written down in the first month after I synced up with "him" in a flood of clarity, inspiration, listening, feeling, and knowing.

It was like I had leveled up in my own first-person video game. And I gained access to a whole cache of gear upgrades in the process.

But there were no cheat codes involved, no shortcuts (although there can be)—just me on my *internal* journey of being curious, open, self-aware, becoming my own observer, taking each level as they came, and doing a lot of internal work along the way to sync up with my higher self.

The funny thing is, in retrospect, it wasn't necessarily "work." When you're "in it" things can feel overwhelming, daunting, challenging, emotional, maybe even impossible. But with each positive decision and each time I pushed through 'veils' of resistance or fear, and each time I followed my intuition or did the hard thing that felt right, I felt better and more complete.

Until, in one profound late-fall afternoon, a few months after my forty-first birthday, over just a few hours, I became whole again.

That was my interpretation of what I experienced "in brief", anyway. For you, I can guarantee that it will be different, as you are not me, and I am not you. Yet, we are all intrinsically connected. This is one of the biggest truths that I experienced when I met My Guy on the 9th Floor.

But this book isn't about me, or him, and it isn't about you either, not your three-dimensional self anyway. It can't be. Because I don't know that expression of you, or the vast collection of experiences, thoughts, feelings, reactions, and emotions that have brought you here, reading or listening to these words in this place, at this time, and in this space. I also don't know your journey.

Only the energetic-you can know what your journey is. Only the energetic-you can know the *feeling* of concepts like expansion and fulfillment because only you can interpret what those words mean for you, and how those concepts feel to you. And only the energetic-you can connect with your *own* expression of what I came to call My Guy on the 9th Floor, once you make the decision to release the layers of conditioning that most of us hold on to so dearly.

This book is about the thoughts, insights, epiphanies, inspirations, connections, tools, practices, and modalities that I have experienced and employed on my own journey that I think can have universal application for those looking for *more* from this life, but not primarily to get something *out* of this life. Because the only way to get something truly valuable out of this life is to look within.

This isn't all new knowledge, but this book *is* a novel approach to putting everything together in a new way that is practical and can be applied by anyone who is ready to get real with themselves in order to create the energetic shifts necessary to change their lives for the better.

This is not a Sprint (but it can be)

There is a chance that as you read the words, concepts, ideas, considerations, and recommendations in this book that you might think to yourself, *"Wow, this sounds amazing,"* or *"Well, duh."*

There is also a chance that even as you are reading this paragraph you might already be dismissing the book outright, or feeling resistance to it, and thinking to yourself, *"This is complete BS; who does this guy freaking think he is?"* (And of course, a multitude of additional reactions, thoughts, feelings, and emotions can be experienced in between.)

If you are in the former camp, that is awesome. High fives all around. I hope there is something new or novel you can take from these words and utilize on your journey.

If you are in the latter camp and are already feeling resistance to the words you're reading in some form (physical, emotional, mental, or spiritual), I encourage you to find a comfortable seat, relax your abdomen to give your diaphragm space to expand, take twelve slow, deep, relaxed, and natural belly breaths, and then ask yourself, *"What do I gain by shutting myself off to thinking differently about my world?"*

Some of us are already "there", fully connected to their source (regardless of their label for it). They are beacons of light and love and peace, and their message is one of connection, understanding, empathy, and acceptance. Some get there quickly. For whatever reason, they were primed and ready to go to make the connection to their higher-self; others perhaps have had an experience of immense contrast and came out the other side looking at their world differently, gaining an additional perspective of their lives.

For me, not so much, at least not at first. My journey has continually evolved, changed, and grown with me. In some ways it has been a lifelong journey, unknowingly priming myself for an accelerated expansion when I was ready. But if I have to put a time frame on the actual *intentional* aspect of this part of my journey, it was probably around three years from where I felt a pull toward something more and getting a first big jolt of "wokeness", to where I was when I got "super woke." During that period of time, there was a *ton* of internal dialogue, internal exploration, internal questioning and being curious about *everything*, self-reflection, self-examination, self-awareness, and radical honesty with myself, that brought me unknowingly ever closer to My Guy on the 9th Floor.

So that's it in a nutshell. This isn't a competition; this isn't a race; you will get "there" exactly when you are supposed to get there, or maybe not. The journey is the goal after all. And we are all on our separate journeys together. The only person in control of your timeline and outcome is you, and the only factor that determines the acceleration of your journey is how ready you are to get radically honest with yourself. Please remember, this type of energetic evolution doesn't have anything to do with anyone but you. It is *only* you.

Take what you need,
leave what you don't,
and enjoy the heck out of your journey.

———————

Choose your own adventure

The next section is about the Foundational Concepts of
Energy (plus Frequency & Vibration),
Zero Point Energy, Quantum Fields, and
our multidimensional world.

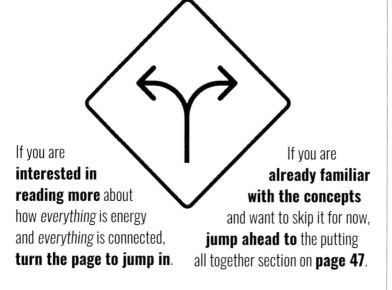

If you are
**interested in
reading more** about
how *everything* is energy
and *everything* is connected,
turn the page to jump in.

If you are
**already familiar
with the concepts**
and want to skip it for now,
jump ahead to the putting
all together section on **page 47**.

Section II

Foundational Concepts

"The first gulp from the glass of natural sciences will make you an atheist, but at the bottom of the glass God is waiting for you."

– Werner Heisenburg
(Father of Quantum Mechanics, Nobel Prize in Physics)

Energy, Frequency, and Vibration

Everything is energy. From the clothes we wear to the cars we drive, and to the thoughts we have, everything has an energetic signature at some level. Some energy is easier to see than others: an illuminated light bulb, a hot stove, a roaring campfire, a bunch of five-year-olds at a birthday party after cake. But energy is the foundation of all things, from the makeup of the universe to the atmosphere of the earth, to the rocks, plants, animals, and us.

Energetic output can be measured in watts, and we are amazingly energetic beings. The average human, at rest, produces around 100 watts of energy. That is equivalent to running a floor fan on high speed. Within a few minutes, or a few hours in the case of trained athletes, we can comfortably sustain 300–400 watts of energetic output (equivalent to running a desktop computer and monitor), and in the case of short bursts of energy, such as sprinting, some humans can output up to 2,000 watts of energy (equivalent to an electric oven baking at 350°F/177°C). And that is just our bodily output. We haven't gotten to the energy of the mind yet.

All energy has a vibrational frequency. Now, since everything is energy, that means that everything has a vibrational frequency. It is the nature of energy; it's always moving even if we can't always perceive it. The specific vibration that any particular form of energy has depends on its energetic—and subsequently, material—makeup. The frequency of energy is calculated using Hertz (Hz), which is a unit of electrical vibration equal to one cycle per second.

Us humans typically have an energetic signature between 62–70Hz when healthy. Which means that, on average, our healthy, resting energetic vibrations cycle between 62–70 times per second. So, because everything is energy, and all energy is naturally vibrational, that means that we are also energetically vibrational by nature. We emit, and we also absorb, energy through our vibrations. We interact with and are influenced by energetic vibrations from our three-dimensional selves (our bodies and our minds, including our thoughts and emotions), other people, the food we eat, our technology and infrastructure, and even our planet because of the vibrational nature of energy.

"Everything in life is vibration." –Albert Einstein

But, how do we know that? How is bodily energy, frequency, and vibration measurable? Beginning with Claude Bernard and Nikola Tesla in the mid-to-late 1800s, and continued with the works of Dr. Royal Raymond Rife in the 1920s, biofeedback has been an area of research that has yielded remarkable insights. The three most common types of biofeedback therapy are:

Thermal biofeedback measures skin temperature.
Electromyography measures muscle tension.
Neurofeedback measures brain wave activity.

Biofeedback enables involuntary responses to be measured and provides us with in-depth knowledge about what is happening in our body.

During biofeedback therapy, electrodes are generally attached to the patient's skin which sends information to measuring equipment.

According to Dr. Rife, every disease has its own specific frequency. The Rife Machine, created by its namesake, was one of the first biofeedback machines. It was a frequency generator that calculated the body's impulses (or frequencies) and communicated the readings through the machine. He found certain frequencies could prevent the development of diseases and others could even destroy them.

Once any bodily imbalances and stresses were identified, the machine's program selected from a database of vibrational biofeedback therapies to help return energetic balance to the bodily system and provide relief for the patient.

In 1934 Dr. Rife's machine was tested on cancer patients at Pasadena County Hospital for ninety days and found that 86.5 percent of the patients had been cured of cancer. The remaining patients underwent additional treatment, were further tested, and they too were cured. **In other words, 100 percent of patients included in the program were cured of cancer.**

According to newspaper and magazine articles[i] of the time, Rife's research, and namesake machine were hits because of the impressive results that they produced. Big pharmaceutical companies tried to buy the technology to conduct more research on his equipment.

Dr. Rife, however, did not want to sell. "When money comes through the door," he said, "science flies out the window."

The short answer to why we are not using biofeedback more broadly to cure disease today is greed and power. The pharmaceutical business is a powerful and profitable industry, and a natural cancer cure such as the Rife Machine would most certainly cut into their margins. After refusing acquisition offers, photos, film, notes, and records began disappearing from his San Diego, California lab. In 1939, a fire destroyed the Burnett Lab in New Jersey, where researchers were about to announce astonishing successes with the Rife Machine, and in 1944 all the records from the Pasadena County Hospital Trials that were being stored at the University of Southern California disappeared.

Luckily the pursuit of biofeedback as a tool to better understand ourselves and our three-dimensional world survived. On the next page are some of the results[ii] of another frequency monitor created by Bruce Tainio of Tainio Technology in 1992.

Energetic Frequencies

The Healthy Body

Brain Frequency Range	72–90 MHz
Genius Brain Frequency	80–82 MHz
Normal Brain Frequency	72 MHz
Human Body	62–78 MHz
Human Body from Neck up	72–78 MHz
Human Body from Neck down	60–68 MHz
Thyroid and Parathyroid glands	62–68 MHz
Thymus gland	65–68 MHz
Heart	67–70 MHz
Lungs	58–65 MHz
Liver	55–60 MHz
Pancreas	60–80 MHz

The Diseased Body

Colds and the Flu start at	57–60 MHz
Disease starts at	58 MHz
Candida overgrowth starts at	55 MHz
Receptive to Epstein Barr at	52 MHz
Receptive to Cancer at	42 MHz
Death begins at	25 MHz

Foods

Fresh Foods	20–27 Hz
Fresh Herbs	20–27 Hz
Dried Foods	15–22 Hz
Dried Herbs	15–22 Hz
Processed/Canned Food	0 Hz

As you can see from the list of readings, things that are healthy (the healthy body: organs, tissue, glands) and things closer to their natural living state (fresh food and herbs) resonate at a higher frequency. Disease and material overly processed or removed from nature resonate at a lower frequency.

Why is this important?

Because each and every one of us has explicit control over our personal vibrational energy. The things we eat; the things we say, think, and feel; and the quality of our minds (optimistic, pessimistic, happy, angry, fearful, resentful, peaceful) all have a direct *energetic* and *vibrational* impact on the quality of our mental, physical, spiritual, and emotional health, as well as our relationship with our world.

"If you want to find the secrets of the universe, think in terms of energy, frequency and vibration."

– Nikola Tesla

Brain Wave Energy

Brain waves have also been measured and seen to have the following frequencies:

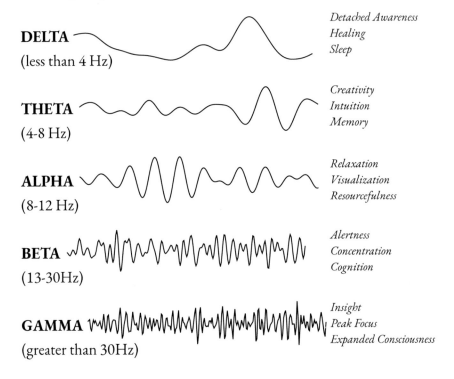

DELTA
(less than 4 Hz)

Detached Awareness
Healing
Sleep

THETA
(4-8 Hz)

Creativity
Intuition
Memory

ALPHA
(8-12 Hz)

Relaxation
Visualization
Resourcefulness

BETA
(13-30Hz)

Alertness
Concentration
Cognition

GAMMA
(greater than 30Hz)

Insight
Peak Focus
Expanded Consciousness

Delta waves have a frequency of around 0.1–4Hz. These waves occur in deep sleep and in some abnormal processes (seizures). It is the dominant rhythm in infants and it is present in sleep stages three and four. Delta waves are the highest in amplitude and the slowest waves. An increase in delta waves creates a decrease in awareness of the physical world (in deep sleep).

Theta waves (measuring around 4–8Hz) are seen in connection with creativity, intuition, daydreaming, and fantasizing, and are a repository for memories, emotions, sensations. Theta waves are strong during internal focus, meditation, prayer, and spiritual awareness. It reflects the state between wakefulness and sleep and relates to the subconscious mind. Theta is a more prevalent brain wave state in children, up to around age thirteen, and then we tend to dip into it less often when awake the older we get. It is also seen when we are in stage one, or light sleep, of the sleep cycle.

Alpha waves measure around 8–12Hz. Good, healthy alpha wave production promotes mental resourcefulness, aids in the ability to mentally coordinate, and enhances an overall sense of relaxation. In this state, we can move quickly and efficiently to accomplish tasks. When alpha waves are predominant, most people feel at ease and calm. It is the major rhythm seen in relaxed adults, and is present most often beyond the age of thirteen when it becomes the dominant brain wave.

Beta waves are fast activity waves, generally resonating between 12–30Hz. Beta waves are dominant in those alert or anxious. Most of the brain is in this state when we are awake and listening and thinking during analytical problem solving, judgment, decision-making, and processing information about the world around us.

Gamma waves are a pattern of normal brain activity that measures between 30–100Hz, with around 40Hz being typical in humans. Gamma brainwaves are the fastest brainwave frequency with the smallest amplitude. This is when our brain waves are oscillating the fastest, and are energetically buzzing or "revved up." It is the brain state most often associated with insight, peak focus, high levels of cognitive function, and expanded states of consciousness. They are also the waves associated with the "feeling of blessings" reported by experienced meditators such as monks and nuns.

Additional work has been done to calculate or quantify the frequency of our less tangible three-dimensional experiences—namely thoughts, emotions, and feelings. The charts on the following pages are visual interpretations of different resonances of *emotional frequency.*

So if everything is energy, and all energy has frequency and resonance, what does that have to do with our experiences here on Earth?

Well, everything. Just like environmental toxins, pollution, and a poor diet can contribute to health issues (by lowering your energetic frequency), *thoughts, feelings, and emotions* can also impact your physical and mental health.

Why isn't more being done to enable us to change our thoughts or emotions, just like I would change my diet if I want to eat healthier? Partly because most people haven't encountered the information, don't have the tools to utilize the information, or haven't experienced a path or plan they can use to make an energetic change.

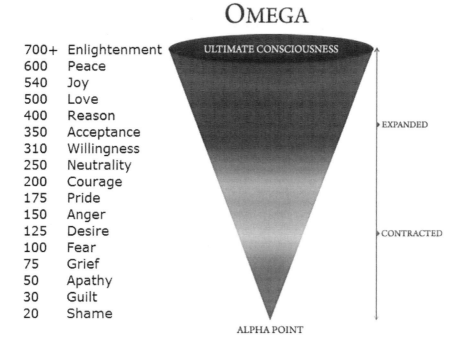

Power Vs. Force: The Hidden Determinants of Human Behavior.[iii]

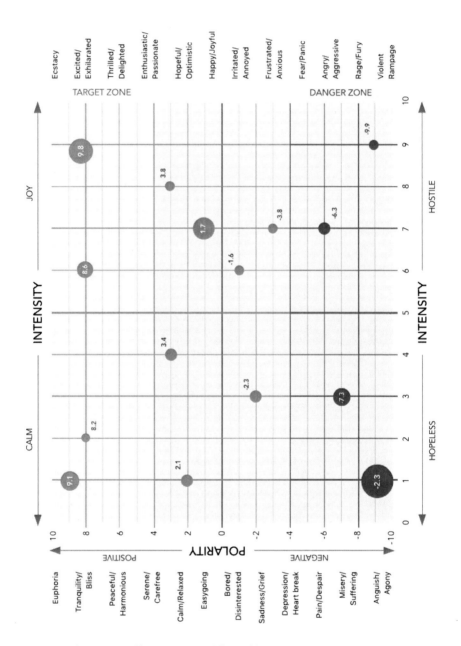

Emotional Frequency Chart courtesy of deanwhitney.com

Also, and more importantly, because feelings, thoughts, and emotions are so darn hard to 'see' and pin down.

We experience them, and then they're gone. It's like continuous, internal "emotional drive-bys" because we are stuck in our three-dimensional experiences but don't have a clear internal perspective *of* our three-dimensional experiences. We get blindsided by emotions, thoughts, and reactions because we are too close to the problem to see it, and too enmeshed with our three-dimensional world to have any objective perspective of it's impact on our lives.

The good news is anyone can improve their vibrational frequency at any time. It's something every single one of us can do. All it takes is the personal decision to begin taking the steps to improve your life from its energetic foundation. So, how do you change your frequency or energetic resonance?

Get outside. Our planet acts like a gigantic electric circuit, and the electromagnetic field of the earth that surrounds and protects all living things has a natural frequency of 7.83Hz. As it turns out, the earth's frequency is not only similar to the alpha brainwave frequency, it is identical to the frequency that control our emotions, thoughts, immune system, and creativity. The more time you can spend outdoors—ideally barefoot, or physically connecting to nature—the better. This is called grounding or earthing. When you are in direct contact with nature, you can more readily connect to the stabilizing frequency of the earth's natural magnetic field. This can help return your general energetic condition to a more centered and balanced state. Forest hikes or walks in the park, swimming in a lake or the ocean (even a pool), running on the beach, building sandcastles with your kids, live action role-playing (LARPing)—whatever your thing is, get outdoors.

Diet. Eat as close to a whole-food, plant-based diet as possible. Avoid overly processed, refined, and/or packaged food as much as possible. Reduce your refined sugar consumption. Eliminate high fructose corn syrup. Bottled juices and smoothies, white bread, bacon, hot dogs, cookies, chips, sugary coffee drinks, sodas, all fast food, and sugary cereals are all examples of foods that do nothing for us energetically. Keep animal protein to a minimum. Also choose locally sourced, humanely raised, naturally-based animal proteins as much as possible. Quality in, quality out. There are myriad resources for help and support in getting started with healthier eating. Get going. You are the only one in control of your life; you are the only one who can decide to start or stop doing something. More information can be found at myguyonthe9thfloor.com/resources.

Exercise. Come on, you guys know this one. Better cardiovascular health, decreased risk for diabetes, boosted mood, increased blood oxygen levels, moving from an acidic to an alkaline state, even changes to how your genes are expressed are all results of physical exertion. Start. Moving. *And* do whatever makes you happy or choose something you want to experience.

Running a 5K, water aerobics, training for a spartan course, frisbee golf, ballroom dancing, basketball, ballet, yoga, doing ten pull-ups in a row, whatever—as long as you're moving, challenge yourself and get going.

Change the quality of your thoughts, emotions, and the way that you are interpreting your three-dimensional and internal spaces. This is the area many of us need the most help with, and is the most crucial yet least explored aspect of health and well-being.

This is where some of us might tune out, because the idea of changing the quality of our thoughts, emotions, and feelings is somewhat of an intangible concept and, for some, hard to visualize. We dive much deeper into it in the *Priming the System: Cleaning the Junk out of the Subconscious Trunk* section of this book, but addressing your subconscious and conscious mind is one of the single most important steps you can take on your journey toward mental, spiritual, emotional, and physical evolution.

Quantum Energy and Quantum Field Theory

Have you ever had an experience where you think about a friend or family member, maybe someone who is close to you but you haven't seen in a while, and shortly after, they call or you run into them somewhere and you reconnect? Do you think this is just pure happenstance, or is there something more going on?

In the previous section, we talked about energy and vibration. Everything is energy, including thoughts, feelings, and emotions. Because your thoughts, feelings, and emotions are energetic, they can have a real-world impact on your physical body, as well as other people's energy in your immediate vicinity, because of the vibrational resonance and frequency of those energies.

But what about at distance?* How can a thought about someone miles away, states or countries or oceans away, influence them in a manor that triggers a response on the other end?

Let's use a version of Occam's Razor, 'the simplest answer is usually the right one', as our benchmark for this thought exploration. Now, create some mental space for yourself and clear out the thoughts. Stop thinking about your to-do list, that cringy person from work, the weird text you got, or anything else.

Quietly to yourself, ask, *"How can a thought about someone miles away, states or countries or oceans away, influence them in a manor that triggers a response?"*

Give yourself a second, but hold on to the first idea that pops into your head when you ask yourself, *"how can someone at distance pick up the phone and call me, just by being thought about?"*

Go ahead and think about that question now.

The first idea that popped into my head was, *"We are all connected in some way."* The simplest answer is usually the right one. Okay, maybe my answer feels right to you, but you might think, *"How can I make sense of it?"*

On the other hand, you might be dismissing the idea outright. If that is the case, I encourage you to again find a comfortable seat, take twelve more deep and relaxed diaphragmatic belly breaths, and ask yourself one more time, *"What do I gain by shutting myself off to thinking differently about my world?"*

How We Are All Connected
Non-Locality/Quantum Entanglement

Niels Bohr, one of the "godfathers" of modern physics, found that once particles (electrons or photons) were in contact, their magnetic orientation remained connected forever, no matter how far in distance they are separated. It has also been observed[iv] that atom communication is faster than the speed of light. When two photons are fired off from a single atom, what happens to one directly and instantly affects the other.

It's been mathematically proven that atoms and molecules are instantaneously and ceaselessly exchanging information inside and outside of our bodies and, well, everywhere. Photons (particles of light) from stars are communicating with every atom they pass on their way to Earth. And at the subatomic level, there is no such thing as empty space. There, in the seemingly finite 'empty' space *within* atoms, is a bubbling sea of quantum field fluctuations that come and go incredibly rapidly, passing *through* atoms, and connecting everything at the subatomic level. Even though we can't see it, our external and internal worlds are teeming with subatomic activity and everything in the universe is energetically connected, including us.

This is the Zero-Point Field of Limitless Energy. It's called zero-point because even at the temperature of absolute zero when all matter should stop moving, there is still activity.

In the 1970s and 1980s, laser physicist Hal Puthoff was trying to figure out how to harness this energy when faced with the fossil fuel crisis. In doing so, he also demonstrated that the zero-point field is responsible for gravity and inertia.[v] All matter in the universe is connected to the zero-point field. All matter is interconnected and entangled through quantum waves. (**This is how the power of thought can be picked up by someone at a distance far away.*)

Researcher R. Ghosh and quantum physicist Anton Zeilinger showed that molecules exist in a 'state of pure potential' until some influence settles them into a more 'complete' state of being. This is illustrated in the Heisenberg Uncertainty Principle which found that in particle physics experiments, the *very act of observing* alters the position of the particle being observed, and makes it impossible (even in theory) to accurately predict its behavior. A good real-world example could be when an interviewee alters their answers to questions in a job interview to align more closely with answers they think will get them the job. Co-creation (observation and reaction to the observation) and influence are the energetic properties of life, and we are constantly co-creating and influencing everything around us, and within us, at the energetic level.

Quantum Field Theory

At its most basic, a quantum field is a connected grid of waves, all potentially in different states of excitation or vibration. There are interactions and energy exchange within the waves of a field based on the different states of the waves. In fact, these waves of energy aren't just waves, they are the 'observable particles' of quantum field theory.

So when we say there is a particle in the field, what we mean is there is an energetic wave of oscillations moving *through* the field that we can see.

Furthermore, because the waves are the observable particles, quantum fields aren't interacting with matter, the waves of a quantum field *are* matter. In other words, the real fundamental fields of nature aren't made of physical things (as far as we can tell); physical things are made of them.

"Everything we call real is made of things that cannot be regarded as real." –Niels Bohr

---

Okay, now this is big-picture thinking about the fabric of everything, so let's take a step back and create a visualization of a connected field. The following is borrowed from physicist Brian Skinner[vi]:

"The first step in creating a picture of a field is deciding how to imagine what the field is made of."

So let's imagine, to start with, that the 'oscillating waves in a state of potential' our quantum field will be made of is represented by a ball at the end of a wound spring.

This is the object we are going to build our field from: an isolated, observable, static wave of matter.

"The field will be composed of an infinite, space-filling array of these ball and springs."

Unfortunately, the previous illustration is fairly static, so the only movement the ball and springs can make is slightly up or down; bobbing is in isolation.

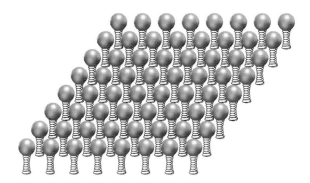

In order to create an actual field, we need to introduce some kind of connection between the balls. So let's imagine adding elastic bands between them.

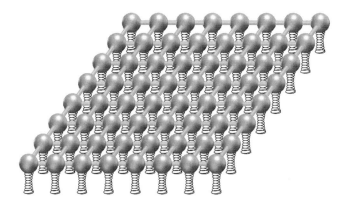

Now, these waves are interacting with each other and we have something that we can legitimately call a field.

If you disturb this field—say, by tapping on it in one area—then it will set off a wave of ball-and-spring oscillations across the field.

These types of fields are part of us. We are all part of these fields, and these fields are the fabric that everything is made of. Also, because everything is energy, any disturbance in a field (say a bad thought about yourself or someone else, or a reactive emotion like anger, fear, or jealousy) has the *potential* to disturb other areas of the field, like our bodies, our minds, or those around us. Everything we do, think, say, feel, and react to has the potential to affect our three-dimensional selves and everything else in our three-dimensional experiences.

Interaction with the Quantum Field - Thought, Intention, and More

The energetic fields that connect everything have the potential to react to any number of our 'energetic expressions', and intention is a great example of this. If you have a strong connection to someone, and a strong thought or intention about or for that person, the energetic output of that thought or intention-experience is magnified. This is because when energies are combined, their total energetic potential is increased.

So if you have positive feelings for someone (love, caring, compassion) and also focus on sending those positive feelings energetically to that person (visualizing the person in your mind and letting yourself feel all the good things you feel for that person), the energetic 'message' is amplified.

In 1994, physicist Elmer Green connected electroencephalogram (EEG) electrodes that were attached to energy healers to a copper wall in order to study the energetic output of the subjects.[vii] They recorded the electrostatic charge when healers sent out their intention.

They found when a person is standing still, heart and breathing show a charge of 10–15 millivolts. When in meditation: 3 volts, and when a healer sends a healing intention: 190 volts.

Researcher and Professor of Materials Science and Engineering at Stanford University, William Tiller did more than 1,000 experiments[viii] that showed thoughts with intention produced a surge in energy, even across distance, up to *50,000 times* the normal rate of an energy pulse detected when there was no intention.

Hal Puthoff also proposed an alternate idea to non-locality. He likened it to two sticks placed in the sand in front of an oncoming ocean wave. It's not that one stick influenced the other stick, it's that a wave/zero-point fluctuation (basically an energy wave) affected both of the sticks. If this is true, then it reinforces the theory that everything in the universe is in touch with every other part of the universe instantaneously.

Additionally, Puthoff suggests if matter is the fluctuations within fields—an underlying ambient, random sea of energy—then it should be possible to use this as a blank matrix on which coherent patterns could be written.

The zero point field has imprinted within it everything that has ever happened through wave interference encoding (remember the light particle interacting with every atom on its journey?). This kind of information might account for 'coherent particles' as well as the field structures themselves.

If we are all connected through these quantum fields of energy, then we could tap into this vast reservoir of energetic information and extract information from it.

But we need to be in the right space to do so and, unfortunately, the three-dimensional space is not it. Fortunately, however, we are not restricted to just our three-dimensional experiences. 😊

Our Multidimensional Lives

How We Experience Third, Fourth, Fifth, and Sixth-Dimensional Energy

"Just like a human fetus, while in the utero, retrieves and assimilates the components that allow its physical body to become whole and fit to emerge into the outer reality, the third dimension serves the purpose of shamanic pregnancy, which is about retrieving and integrating the fragmented pieces of the soul, finally giving birth to the multidimensional self."

– Franco Santoro

One of the biggest distinctions the ideas in this book makes is between the limited perceptual "reality" of what we can experience in our three-dimensional world, and the expansive dimensions of energy, frequency, and vibration that connect all things within our three-dimensional world and beyond.

Here is my interpretation of the different energetic dimensions we experience as humans, and how they play into the concept of being conscious, consciousness, and higher consciousness.

The third dimension is everything that we can experience with our 'worldly' receptors: our senses, our body, our conscious mind, and our subconscious mind. Our conscious and subconscious minds are part of our three-dimensional world because they are *subjective* to our three-dimensional experiences. *All* human life experiences, history, exploration, thoughts, feelings, emotions, reactions, stories, the observable universe, and systems of contrast (government, monetary, social, entertainment) are *of* our three-dimensional experiences. This is the conscious world.

We are here to experience the contrasts of our three-dimensional world in all its beauty, glory, and messiness, and seeming complexity, difficulty, and every other adjective that we can come up with. And we are here to release resistance to all of the contrast we experience. By experiencing contrast and *releasing resistance* to the contrast we experience in our three-dimensional lives, we increase the capacity of our individual energetic bodies to expand, fostering a more peaceful, present, and centered space internally.

By experiencing the contrast of our three-dimensional lives, but *holding onto resistance to that contrast*, we create disease, disharmony, and disruption in our energetic bodies (physically, mentally, spiritually, and emotionally).

You can think of an energetic fourth-dimension as the expansive interior space within your mental landscape. Labels like 'fourth-dimensional thinking' and 'out-of-the-box' thinking are referring to this internal space of expansion, creativity, honesty, joy, and peacefulness. The place where you can observe three-dimensional thoughts, emotions, and reactions instead of feeling like you are subjective to them. This is the space where you can experience everything as well as cultivate non-resistance to everything. A place connected to our three-dimensional world, but not *of* our three-dimensional world.

This is where the state of being conscious intermingles with consciousness, or the state of awareness that you are a conscious being. This is where you, as the Observer of your three-dimensional experiences, can grow. Where you can begin to access aspects of your soulful self. This is also the place of energetic connection to your heart, the positive 'voice in your head', and a conduit to your balanced and empathetic center.

The fifth dimension is pure energy that we, as energetic beings, are connected to, part of, can influence, and are influenced by. This is the quantum realm. Quantum energy fields, energetic vibrational resonance and frequency, Oort fields, chakras, collective consciousness, and auras are all part of the energetic connection layer coursing through everything in the universe. Not an isolated dimension, but one that permeates and is enmeshed with all things. This is the energetic fabric that is integrated with everything we can perceive with our 'worldly' receptors, as well as everything beyond what we can perceive.

I have personally experienced interactions with collective consciousness more frequently since I began my journey. Sometimes, with the energy work I was doing, an answer to a question eluded me, or there was a message that I needed to receive to resolve a condition I was experiencing, and the information or message could be found in a random book on a shelf, or in a magazine, and even one time on a hotel policy and procedures sheet. The information is there if we just open ourselves to finding it in ways we might never consider with strictly three-dimensional thinking. Collective consciousness and quantum energy can also be contributing factors in concepts like parallel development. The emergence of pyramids as a building structure around the globe, or Roger Bannister breaking the four-minute mile barrier are both prime examples. As soon as either event happened, that knowledge became part of a collective, connected grid of information, and both pyramid structures and sub-four-minute mile times increased around the world.

I have also experienced our connected, collective energetic field of information in more unexpected and personal ways.

The first one was mine. I was on a flight with my parents when I was young, maybe four or five years old. The flight attendant came on the PA system with a trivia game to win a prize. Whoever could guess correctly would win a bottle of champagne. (Hey, it was the 1980s.)

The question was, "What was the distance of the Wright Brothers' *longest first flight*?" I remember asking myself the question in my head a few times slowly. And then, seemingly out of nowhere, a number popped into my mind. It wasn't a guess—I felt it in my body like when you hear an absolute truth, I knew it. The number just came to me. I told one of my parents that I knew the answer, so they told me to raise my hand. I did, and I told the flight attendant the number. That correct answer, that I hadn't known before that moment, ended up winning my parents a bottle of champagne.

The other is from my daughter. She was about a year and a half old, and was sitting on our counter 'helping' my wife clean our herb and spice rack. My wife had all the jars of spices on the counter and was wiping them down to put back in their places. She and our daughter were talking, and when she picked up the ginger to put it back, our daughter said, "That's for the eyes", and pointed to her eye. My wife smiled, and responded with something along the lines of, "No sweetie, not for eyes. This is for flavor, we use this for food." A few minutes later as my wife was putting away another jar, our daughter pointed and said, "That's good for ears."
My wife, smiling again, reassured her "No honey, this one's not for the ears. This is thyme, we also use it flavor to food."

Hearing the insistence and sincerity in our young daughter's words, the interaction stuck with my wife and, a few days later, she decided to look up household herbs that were good for both the eyes and ears. It turns out that ginger is an anti-inflammatory that can be used to treat inflammation of the middle-eye and thyme has been used traditionally to treat infections and earaches.

Where does this knowledge come from? How did my daughter and I not think about or learn, but *know* those things? The only thing that makes sense to me is an interconnected, energetic field of information to which we are all connected, and we are all a part of. Quantum energy isn't some esoteric concept or shrouded mysticism or something that we can only 'know' after leaving our three-dimensional world, but something that each and every one of us is vibrantly connected to, and that we can utilize to more strongly connect to our energetic-selves.

The energetic sixth dimension is spiritual energy. Spirit, God, Source, Alpha and Omega, whatever you call the collective good of 'us.' This is our origin. Where we come from and to where we all return. We are all a part of it, it is our energetic core, and it is a part of everything we can perceive with our three-dimensional receptors.

Everything is connected.

Putting it all Together

Everything is made of energy, including us.

Energy is vibrational in nature.

Even seemingly solid matter is alive with vibrational energy at some level.

We can measure energetic output by looking at the different frequencies that energetic vibrations have.

The 'particles' that can be observed in a Quantum field are actually the signature of *the energy waves moving through the field.*

Because of the nature of energetic waves moving through quantum fields, everything is connected.

From the makeup of the universe, to every element of our planet, and even us.

Everything is connected energetically to everything else.

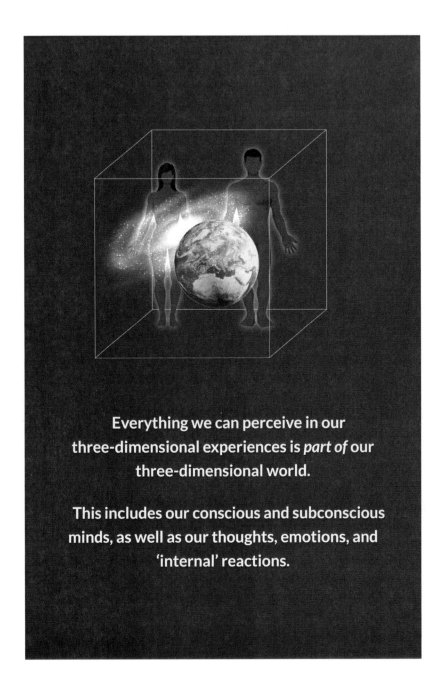

Everything we can perceive in our three-dimensional experiences is *part of* our three-dimensional world.

This includes our conscious and subconscious minds, as well as our thoughts, emotions, and 'internal' reactions.

The more enmeshed we are with our
three-dimensional experiences, the more
subjective we are to our experiences and the
more (dis)ease and resistance to contrast we will
likely experience.

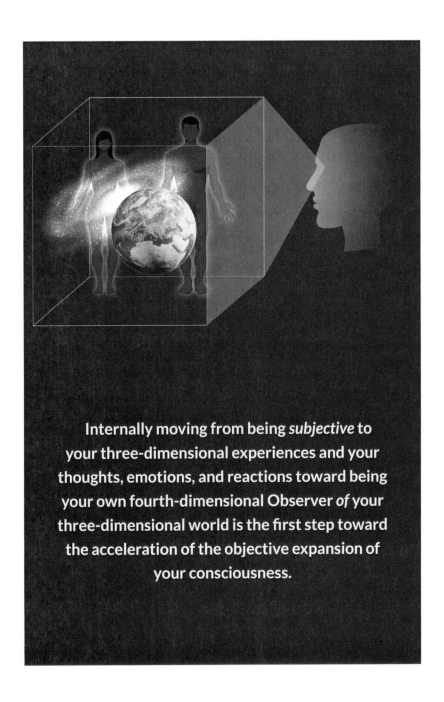

Internally moving from being *subjective* to your three-dimensional experiences and your thoughts, emotions, and reactions toward being your own fourth-dimensional Observer *of* your three-dimensional world is the first step toward the acceleration of the objective expansion of your consciousness.

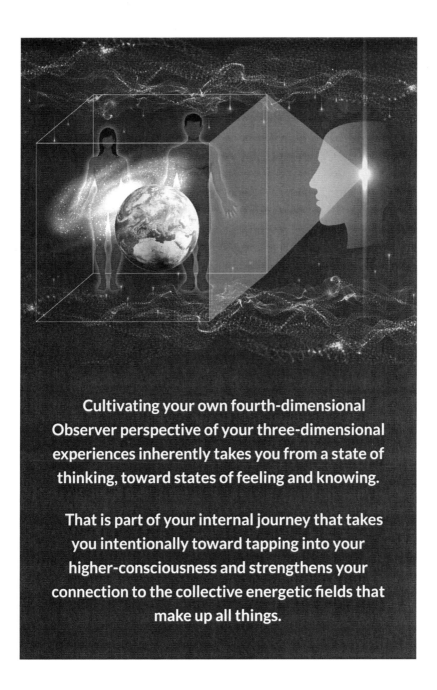

Cultivating your own fourth-dimensional Observer perspective of your three-dimensional experiences inherently takes you from a state of thinking, toward states of feeling and knowing.

That is part of your internal journey that takes you intentionally toward tapping into your higher-consciousness and strengthens your connection to the collective energetic fields that make up all things.

Section III

Our Three-Dimensional World:
A 10,000-Foot View

"The world we have created is a product of our thinking; it cannot be changed without changing our thinking.

If we want to change the world we have to change our thinking...no problem can be solved from the same consciousness that created it.

We must learn to see the world anew."

– Ram Dass / Albert Einstein

Prisoners of Our Own Design: Addicted to the Contrast,
Codependent on the Resistance

Economic, political and social systems, religion, monetary systems, technology, *any* grouping system (for example: racism), heck, even sports teams or college affiliation are all three-dimensional constructs we have created that rely on separation for strength, and difference and contrast for validation.

Good versus bad, capitalism versus socialism, Democrat versus Republican, Muslim versus Christian, traditional currency versus cryptocurrency, Apple versus Samsung, Liverpool versus Manchester United, Michigan versus Ohio State, my experiences versus *my perception* of your experiences—none of them would have the power that we *think* they have without our 100 percent tacit consent and addiction to the feedback that we get from those three-dimensional systems.

The closer someone is to the spectrum-edge of any system (the 'extreme' views) the more contrast they will experience and the *less* likely they will be able to release resistance to what they observe at the opposite end of the spectrum. This is the place where resentment, hate, fear, anger, hostility, and separation are born.

It is impressive how powerful the energy behind our entanglement with our three-dimensional systems can be. The *only* reason the US dollar has remained a benchmark for global currency as long as it has is due to collective belief. Yet we still doubt that we are powerful creators of our own world.

In the 'bigger than us' sense, the only reason we are here is to experience the contrasts of our three-dimensional world and release resistance to those contrasts. That's it. But because we get so caught up with, enamored by, or imprisoned in the different states of contrast that we experience, and because most of us don't know or haven't been exposed to anything *but* our three-dimensional world, we lose any semblance of *internal* perspective other than what we can perceive with our three-dimensional receptors: (1) Our senses and our bodies, (2) the conscious mind, and (3) the subconscious mind.

By not providing ourselves any *internal space* to observe our three-dimensional world *slightly apart* from our three-dimensional perceptions (this is moving into the state of becoming your own Observer), we are signing our own life sentence of imprisonment and distress, resistance and struggle. Feelings of depression or anxiousness, many psychological disorders, 'working for the weekend', physical/emotional/substance abuse, and hatred are all *symptomatic expressions* of (dis)ease in our energetic systems that stem from being too enmeshed with our experiences. We are too close to the problem to objectively see any 'solution' to those symptoms of (dis)ease other than three-dimensional ones.

And the only 'being-entangled-in-the-three-dimensional-experience' solution seemingly available to many of us is to mask the symptoms we experience with medication in one form or another. Prescription drugs, illegal drugs, entertainment binging, social media, alcohol abuse, dangerous behavior, eating disorders, seeking external approval/validation, and violence are all examples of 'medications' we use to mask symptoms of (dis)ease whose actual energetic cause is seemingly out of our grasp.

It is our internal, energetic-self knowing something is wrong, but our *subconscious* minds having no other way to communicate that something is wrong to our *conscious* mind than to speak through physical, mental, and psychological channels. Our internal-selves are screaming at us that something is wrong; there is disharmony and (dis)ease taking place in the bodily system, and all we can do is address the *symptom*, not the root cause, because most of us have never been taught anything other than what we can perceive three dimensionally.

It's like we reactively lunge for the remote to turn off the TV the second an emergency warning starts to play and think, *"Should I look at what that alert is about? Nope, not gonna open myself up to diving deeper into whatever that is. I just want the noise to stop!"*

We are so immersed in our three-dimensional experiences that we can't see the forest for the trees. And in that state, it is hard for us to see what living a fulfilled life in our three-dimensional world could, or should, be.

A Brief Additional Word About Religion

In some ways, most (if not all) religions do get it 'right' to some extent. Some of the messages that have been passed down over the centuries *are* reflective of a journey inward toward your own personal, elevated relationship with whatever you call the energy that is greater than 'us.'

'Treat others how you want to be treated', 'take care of those who need it', 'to know God is to know yourself'—the core messages are there, but problems arise when concepts and ideas that are bigger than our three-dimensional experiences, but have been modified *in* our three-dimensional world, are applied *to* our three-dimensional experiences. Because the works of elevated individuals and messages of 'the word' have been translated, rewritten, changed, omitted, modified, and interfered with through the ages, they have inherently been adulterated from the core messages of pure love, compassion, and empathy to include three-dimensional concepts like separation (us versus them), fear (fear of the unknown, fear of death, fear of not being 'saved'), and guilt (the concept of being born into sin).

This is why it is hard for a strictly three-dimensional thinker to experience the world any other way when they are *in* their three-dimensional experiences but don't realize they are not *of* their three-dimensional experiences. This is where difference, separation, and contrast—instead of being experienced and released—has been clung to, and the grooves of difference have been dug deeper and deeper in our psyche. Where there are messages of peace, unity, and harmony, there are also messages of superiority, separateness, control, and division, and that theirs is the only way to 'salvation.'

For better or worse, and regardless if the *intent* behind the interference was benevolent, benign, or malevolent, the messages have been used to serve the organizations and individuals in perceived places of power, as opposed to purely serving the individuals they are supposed to lead and inspire.

Why do I say, "perceived places of power"? Because no one has any power over anyone else, unless that power is given. No one can take anything from the energetic-you.

There is no one 'right way' or single righteous path other than the path that is the one-right-way for you.

These vehicles that are intended as messages of peace and salvation have been manipulated and adulterated because the only lens we have been viewing them through is an external, three-dimensional one. Some examples of similar messages from Hinduism, Christianity, and Islam:

The essence of Hinduism is the same essence of all true religions: Bhakti or pure love for God [yourself connection to your higher-self] and genuine compassion for all beings.
— Radhanath Swami

Know ye not that ye are the temple of God, and that the Spirit of God dwelleth in you?
1 Cor. 3:16

Test yourselves to see if you are in the faith; examine yourselves!
Or do you not recognize this about yourselves, that Jesus Christ is in
you—unless indeed you fail the test?
2 Cor. 13:15

The Quran presents the universe as a model, which is characterized
by harmony and peace. When God created heaven and earth, He so
ordered things that each part might perform its function peacefully
without clashing with any other. The Quran tells us that "It is not
allowable (i.e., possible) for the sun to reach the moon, nor does the
night overtake the day, but each, in an orbit, is swimming."
(Surah 36:40)

The messages are all there, across the board.

If you are currently *of* a religion, and the experience leaves you
feeling peaceful, joyful, energized, and fulfilled, and you are able to
view our three-dimensional world as the objective observer instead
of the subjective experiencer, and you engage with anything that
anyone else in your world does, thinks, or says from an objective
place without attachment, and you live your life with radical
honesty, and acceptance, and balance, and empathy . . . fantastic!
Keep on keepin' on. And keep reading to potentially experience
even more contrast and the opportunity to release resistance to
that contrast.

If you are currently *of* a religion, and you are experiencing fear,
anger, resentment or hatred of the 'other', sadness, unfulfillment,
looking outside of yourself for 'answers', questioning things, or

thinking these words I'm writing are bull-honkey . . . fantastic.
Keep reading. You are in the perfect place to begin your journey
deeper into yourself, gaining a better understanding of who you are
beyond your three-dimensional experiences, and getting to a place
of being able to experience the contrasts of life and letting.
Them. All. Go.

The Story of the Elephant

There is a story about a man who, as he was passing a group of
elephants, suddenly stopped, confused by the fact that these huge
creatures were being held by only a small rope tied to their front
leg. No chains, no cages. It was obvious that the elephants could,
at any time, break away from their bonds but for some reason, they
did not.

He saw a trainer nearby and asked why these animals stood still
and made no attempt to escape. "Well," the trainer said, "when
they are very young and much smaller, we use the same size rope to
tie them and, at that age, it's enough to hold them. As they grow
up, they are conditioned to believe they cannot break away. They
believe the rope can still hold them, so they never try to break free."

This is one of my all-time favorite parables. It resonated with me
from the moment I first read it. I think this is a close, but not exact,
approximation to the human three-dimensional experience.
The main difference being that our shackles are invisible and we
were never even aware that we were imprisoned to begin with.

Begin by Allowing Yourself to Experience
Contrast Without Resistance

The first decision you have to make once you have begun your journey is to acknowledge there could be something beyond your perceptual view of our three-dimensional world and that, maybe, the 'systems' we have created to serve us could be the very things that we have allowed to shackle us. You don't even have to believe it, just entertain the idea at first.

If you can remove yourself just slightly from your immediate three-dimensional enmeshment, you might just find a little space to look at the experience more objectively, instead of feeling like you are being subjected to it.

Here's an exercise. Think about a 'situation of contrast' that you have recently experienced. Make it something that initiated an emotional, thought, or reactive response. A fight with a family member, an argument with a partner, the person that cut you off in traffic, a difficult co-worker or boss, your child who was 'acting out' — whatever it is for you.

Think about the situation, and let yourself feel all the resistance that you might be hanging on to about it. Anger, resentment, frustration, fear, hurt, sadness—again, whatever the 'label' is for you.

Now, while you are still feeling the resistance find a comfortable seat in a chair, cross your legs at the ankles, cross your arms at the wrists with your thumbs pointing down, clasp your hands, and close your eyes.

This is called a hook-up (or whole-brain) posture, where both hemispheres of your brain are active and balanced. You are going to take twelve full, natural, and relaxed belly breaths, and as you are moving through your breaths let any resistance you still have to the situation of contrast melt away. Let it all go. Allow yourself to release any negative thoughts, feelings, or emotions that you may still be clinging to about the situation, other people involved in the situation, and even yourself, and let it all go with your exhalations. Allow yourself to have experienced the situation of contrast, and allow yourself to move into an internal place of non-resistance to it. If you are still experiencing any resistance to the situation, move through additional rounds of belly breaths, remaining in the whole brain posture.

Alternatively, if 'release through breath' hasn't alleviated the feelings of resistance internally, you can try turning *into* the negative feelings, and burning them out, instead of letting them flow away. If this is you, let yourself feel whatever the label is for you (anger, resentment, frustration, fear, hurt, sadness) and let yourself turn up the intensity of that negative emotion internally. Anger? Ball up your hands, flex every muscle in your body, squeeze your eyes as tight as you can and 'burn out' all of the anger you feel (you can scream into a pillow too if you need additional release). Sadness? Don't turn away from it, or shut the feeling down, or just bottle it up inside.

Seated Hook-up (or Whole Brain) Posture. Arms and legs crossed, hands clasped with fingers interlaced and thumbs pointing down. Hands can remain in lap or, with hands clasped, fold arms under and up so elbows point down and pinky fingers rest against upper chest. This posture can also be used laying down.

Steer into the sadness and let yourself experience it completely to move through it. Let yourself cry. Let yourself bawl like a baby. Let yourself wail and get snotty. If the experience burns out the sadness, but something else arises, keep going if you can. Steer into the next negative feeling that arises and burn that one out too.

If, after a few rounds of breathing, or turning into the negative feelings you are still feeling strong resistance or are unable to find any internal distance from the situation and are having a hard time letting go of your reactions, thoughts, or emotions, please read the *Priming the System* section of this book for additional tools and insights.

You are Not Your Thoughts, Emotions, or Reactions

Read this next part out loud:

"I am not my thoughts."

"I am not my emotions."

"I am not my reactions."

Once more (this part is important), but this time only say the words in your head:

"I am not my thoughts."

"I am not my emotions."

"I am not my reactions."

Embodying these statements and letting the realization that you are not these things resonate within you is the beginning of creating internal distance between the energetic-you and your three-dimensional self.

Thoughts, emotions, and reactions are part of our subconscious minds, and are continually influenced and impacted by the rest of our three-dimensional world, but they are not part of the energetic-you. They are here for the energetic-you to experience and release resistance to.

Now it might feel like thoughts, emotions, and reactions are all 'in your head' or separate from your three-dimensional world, but remember everything is connected energetically. The seemingly intangible energy of thoughts, feelings, and reactions can also be felt around you, and will affect things outside of your head—your body, your friends, your family, people in your community, and the entire planet.

Have you ever walked into a room and felt 'good vibes', or walked into a different room after a fight has just occurred and felt ill-at-ease, like there is static in the air? Those are both examples of your energetic field interacting with other people's energetic fields, and even when the energy isn't *consciously* recognized, it is *constantly* influencing our experiences as well as the experiences of those around us.

Thoughts, emotions, and reactions are some of the most powerful forces on Earth. When enough people start thinking, emoting, or reacting in a similar way, it can have massive local, regional, and even global impact, regardless of whether it is 'good' or 'bad', because concepts of 'good' and 'bad' are parts of our three-dimensional systems as well, and are inherently subjective.

Language is another very powerful tool in the toolbox that we have created to help us perceive and experience the contrast of our three-dimensional world.

Becoming a Steward of Your Internal Space

Now just because you are not your thoughts, emotions, and reactions, doesn't let you off the hook to live a debaucherous, hedonistic lifestyle. It actually ups the ante. Because now that you realize, or are maybe starting to consider, you are not your thoughts, emotions, and reactions means you (and only you) have the power over, and responsibility for, the *quality of your mind* when you experience the contrasts of our three-dimensional world.

Only you can choose to let go of resistance and keep all of your three-dimensional experiences in their place: as things to be experienced, considered, and released, but not to become enmeshed with or beholden to. Only you can choose to start living a purposeful life, one that is meaningful and fulfilling to you and you alone. Because no one else is playing your video game, no one else can 'beat' your levels and move forward on your journey, and no one else can grow and evolve your life except you.

Consider Everything in Your Three-Dimensional Experience an Opportunity for Increasing Contrast, Reducing Resistance, and Beginning to Observe. Look at all media, opinion, artistic expression, and every other form of system in our world as tools of contrast that you can utilize on your journey of expansion. If you can experience *contrast without resistance* in your mind, whether the contrast you experience is 'good' or 'bad', you are growing as a being.

Reactive states of judgment, condescension, meanness, anger, dismissiveness, fear, self-abuse, depression, anxiety, scarcity, or jealousy are all byproducts of being in a state of resistance, and only serve to keep you a prisoner of your three-dimensional perceptions of the world.

The flaws, shortcomings, annoyances, or negative attributes you see in others is only the universe holding up a mirror to yourself and reflecting areas ripe for release and expansion. Anything you have a strong reaction to is an opportunity for greater awareness, more honest reflection/observation, and to take a different action/ have a different reaction than you have in the past.

Next, Consider Nothing Anyone Else Does in Your Three-Dimensional World Has Anything to Do With You. Have you ever thought something like, *"My kids are driving me crazy,"* or *"My partner makes me so mad,"* or *"I can't stand [insert name]. They think they are so much better than everyone else,"* or *"How dare you say that; you are triggering me,"* or *"My partner is cheating. I can't believe they would do that to me"*?

Those are all illusions of being immersed *in* your three-dimensional experience without the perspective to *see* the three-dimensional world for what it is. No one else in your experiences can make you feel, think, or do anything. You are the only one in control of your inner space, as well as your interactions with your three-dimensional world.

Your kids 'acting out' are experiencing their own contrast and exploring their own worlds. Your partner is living in *their* expression of our shared world and reacting to their experiences with whatever resistance or misfiring subconscious programs are influencing their three-dimensional receptors. That person who you can't stand is playing *their* version of their own first-person video game. Whoever is saying 'triggering' things is living in their own perception of our world, and has no idea what your 'triggers' are. The cheating partner is in a *deep* place of resistance to their own (dis)ease whose symptoms have expressed themselves through infidelity, but all of these examples have nothing to do with *you*. This is part of radical empathy.

You may be feeling resistance to this idea, or having a strong three-dimensional reaction to the concept. Or you may be open to considering it or have already assimilated it, but yes, this can be a challenging concept to entertain.

It is a concept that may seem counterintuitive at first. It is also one that many of us balk at, have trouble reconciling, or downright refuse to consider as soon as personal examples are applied to it. But the fact remains that you cannot control, nor are you responsible for, or a victim of, anyone else's behavior, thoughts, or actions.

The more space you can give yourself to practice the concepts that: a) you are not your thoughts, emotions, and reactions, and b) nothing anyone else does has anything to do with you... the faster you will be able to move away from being subjective to the experiences in your life toward becoming the *objective* observer of your world, and letting go of resistance much more easily and more quickly, creating a healthier you and a healthier planet.

The Car and the Driver

We are all experiencing our three-dimensional world as the car and not the driver.

Every bump, every pothole, all the miles on the tires and wear and tear on the engine, transmission, shocks, brakes, and electrical system are felt much more visceral because we think we are the car. The more we realize that we are not our thoughts, emotions, and reactions, the better equipped we will be to *drive* the car as opposed to *embodying* the car being driven. As we begin to move into the driver's seat, we are moving into a state of observation and energetic connection that takes us even further away from the perceived impact our three-dimensional experiences can have on us, eventually arriving at a place where we aren't even driving the car anymore. We move to a place of being/knowing where we can begin to embody the **player** *playing the game that the car and driver are part of.*

Move from being enmeshed with thoughts and feelings (you are the car), to observing them (you are the driver observing the car being driven), and then to a state of presence, intuition, being, and knowing (you are the player playing the first-person video game that the car and driver are part of).

How do you move from thinking to knowing, from being the car to becoming the driver and beyond?

At first, it is all about awareness. Awareness of reactions, feelings, and thoughts that originate from stimuli in the three-dimensional world.

If you have a reactive negative experience, and afterward think something to the effect of: *"Oh man, that was a crazy [reaction, emotion, thought]; that didn't feel good!"* That is recognition. The faster you move through reaction to recognition, the faster you are moving toward observational awareness of your interactions with your world.

Then it is about reflection. *"Why did I have that reaction? Where did that come from? Why do I keep having these same thoughts, emotions, and reactions?"* Creating space between yourself and your thoughts, emotions, and reactions can help you identify your own internal blind spots and is the first step to moving into the driver's seat of your car. This is the beginning of a new radically honest relationship with yourself and can be uncomfortable. If it is uncomfortable or challenging to observe your emotions, thoughts, or reactions, and to take responsibility for them and release resistance to the negative, you are not alone.

This is often one of the most challenging (albeit ultimately rewarding) steps in your journey. Moving through resistance and allowing yourself to feel discomfort internally, and then releasing those feelings can take you to places you might not expect.

A reaction toward a partner can have its roots in relationships from adolescence or a confrontation from your youth that you've forgotten about. A conflict with a boss or coworker can have its energetic roots in a relationship with a parent. An inability to 'move forward' in life can be linked to a traumatic experience your subconscious mind has assimilated into your daily life. But the more open, honest, curious, kind, and reflective you can be with your energetic-self, the closer you will be moving toward freedom from your three-dimensional experiences.

And lastly, it is about action and taking the steps to change your perceptual reality to begin moving into the 'player of the game' vantage point. More on how to do that is up next.

Section IV

Priming the System: Becoming the Observer of Your Own Fourth-Dimension

"Each of the small enlightenments that a Zen practitioner has, which are known in Zen as "Satori experiences," provides deeper insights into the nature of existence and helps a person prepare for complete enlightenment."

— Frederick Lenz

Stagnation is an Illusion;
You are Always Moving Toward Something

Have you ever felt stuck in life? Stuck in a job, stuck in a relationship, stuck in a friend group, stuck in depression or anxiety, stuck in resistance to ways of thinking that challenge your world view, stuck in grief? Well, the reality is, again because everything is energy, the perceived experience of feeling 'stuck' is just an illusion. Energy is inherently in a constant state of movement, even if we can't perceive it. Because everything is energetically connected, this creates a spectrum of vibrational potential just waiting to be influenced by an external force, both the good and the bad.

So what you are experiencing when you feel stuck or stagnant is not the absence of movement or momentum, but it is the repeated pattern of connecting energetically to an undesirable 'force' over and over again, even if it is a 'force' at the subconscious level. It is like being caught in a feedback loop.

You are always moving toward something, even if the thing you are moving toward is the thing you are trying to get away from.

Because if you are operating at the thing-you-are-trying-to-get-away-from's energetic frequency, you will attract more of that thing to you. It is up to you (and only you) to decide what you are moving toward and, if needed, take the steps to change your path internally.

The only way you can truly affect your three-dimensional experience is to *enhance your capacity for expanding internal space* between your energetic-self and your three-dimensional receptors in preparation to move definitively into your own internal fourth-dimensional experience as the Observer.

Finding distance between your energetic-self and your three-dimensional experiences is a massive step on the journey toward connecting to your energetic 'higher' self (which, again, expresses itself individually for each and every one of us). This is where the **internal dialogue, internal exploration, internal questioning, self-reflection, self-examination, self-awareness**, and *radical honesty* with self comes more and more into play.

Now, while you are not your thoughts, emotions, and reactions, *becoming aware of and directing your attention toward the origins* of your thoughts, emotions, and reactions through all of the practices I just listed is the next massive step toward becoming your own Observer.

Cleaning the Junk out of the Subconscious Trunk

Our subconscious minds are incredibly powerful things. By some accounts, we are only consciously aware of about 5 percent of what we are thinking, feeling, and reacting to on any given day. The other 95 percent (some researchers suggest as much as 98 percent) of the time, our subconscious programs are running the show.

All of our involuntary, bodily/systemic actions (the autonomic nervous system: breathing, heartbeat, digestive functions) as well as our three-dimensional drives, impulses, fears, instincts, emotions, reflexes, and reactive behaviors are controlled by the subconscious mind. Additionally, the subconscious mind is the repository of every single experience you have ever had, even since before you were born.

Every experience, emotion, stimulus, thought—everything you have ever perceived, whether consciously or not—in your three-dimensional world is stored in your subconscious mind. In this way, your subconscious mind operates like a quantum supercomputer that has been writing programs and software since you were in utero. Now, this supercomputer is exceptionally powerful, and its only purpose is to keep you safe in your three-dimensional world. There are a lot of things in our world that can physically, emotionally, spiritually, or mentally affect us, and it is the subconscious' job to protect us.

Unfortunately, our subconscious supercomputers are too good at their jobs and also pretty bad at situational awareness.

Post Traumatic Stress Disorder (PTSD) is a good example of when a program of 'safety' in the subconscious mind is run outside of the situation in which it was created. Pretty much anything can cause a traumatic experience to 'get stuck', but let's use a military example since those can be at the more extreme end of the contrast spectrum.

Imagine you are deployed, and you and your squad are in the shit. Enemy fire coming from multiple locations, pinned down, fighting where you can and hoping for support or withdrawal. Miraculously, it comes and your squad makes it out.

In this 'in the shit' situation, your conscious mind is in the moment; it is calculating firing vectors, visualizing the terrain and cover, assessing vulnerabilities, and dozens of additional factors. The *subconscious* mind is running your training programs, triggering physical and mental reactions, releasing adrenaline, keeping you breathing, and beating your heart. But, it is also simultaneously writing new programs, in real time, based on the current experiences. Like I said, this is one powerful machine.

Now you've finished your tour and you're back home. You are no longer in bodily danger, you are no longer wondering if you are going to make it out alive, or experiencing rounds impacting all around you. But if your *subconscious mind* is somehow brought back to that experience (maybe you happened to think about it, or you hear a car backfire, or maybe you see someone with a suspicious bulge under their shirt or reconnect with people in your squad, or it wells up within you, or any number of additional three-dimensional experiences that can trigger a subconscious response), your subconscious mind activates the programs that were written when you were in it, because to your subconscious, those programs are what kept you safe.

What you are experiencing is an outdated program that no longer serves its purpose, running in a context that it was not intended for. That is why PTSD can be so debilitating and devastating. The program is stuck in a loop, your subconscious mind keeps running it because it thinks it's helping, but it wreaks havoc on your conscious mind and the rest of your current three-dimensional world. And each time the program runs, it becomes more and more embedded in the system.

Another way to think about it is like grooves on a record. Each time the record plays the grooves get deeper and more pronounced.

Until we are about seven years old, we are primarily building the supercomputer, writing code, and downloading programs based on the world around us. How our parents treat us, how they treat each other, all the playing and observation, and just being alive; we are literally soaking up everything we experience like a sponge. From the age of seven on up, our operating system boots up and runs the programs it has written, as well as the ones it continues to perpetually write.

Now, every program that we have ever written operates exactly as intended, but maybe not always when you want them to, especially the older we get and the more programs and software patches we add to the supercomputer.

Subconscious programs running in situations they were not intended for and/or that no longer serve us are one of the biggest contributing factors to the (dis)ease we experience in our three-dimensional worlds.

From a processing standpoint, conservative estimates put the capacity of our conscious minds at around 40 bits/second while our subconscious minds are operating at closer to 20,000,000 bits/second.

Let that sink in. Our subconscious minds are operating, conservatively, at *500,000 times* the capacity of our conscious minds.

How on Earth could we ever think there is any way we can 'out-think', 'out-intention', or 'consciously outmaneuver' a supercomputer with what equates to a pocket calculator? That is like putting a penny on a train track with the *hope* that the penny will derail the train; it just won't happen. How could we ever change anything internally with *just* 'positive thoughts', or 'only good vibes' and 'no bad days' ways of thinking?

Okay, so now we have some analogous information to work from so we can deepen our understanding of what our options are in dealing with this obstacle of almost built-in 'programs of resistance' and 'non-acceptance.' A massive supercomputer running things automatically 95–98 percent of the time on the one side, and a conscious-mind-pocket-calculator-equivalent on the other. So what do we do? What is the simplest way forward in this scenario?

The Supercomputer of You

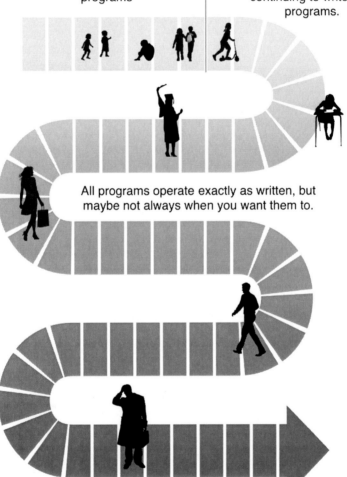

Ages 0-7

The subconscious mind is absorbing *everything*, writing code, and downloading programs

~ Ages 7+

The 'operating system of you' boots up and runs the programs it has created *as well as* continuing to write new programs.

All programs operate exactly as written, but maybe not always when you want them to.

The Subconscious vs. The Conscious Mind

Subconscious Mind

Conditioned responses,
autonomic processes, and
the repository ot everything
you've ever experienced.

**being used ~95%
of the time**

Conscious Mind

Critical thinking, reasoning,
sensations, perceptions,
memories, feeling, and
fantasies inside of our
current awareness

**only used ~5% of
the time**

Processing Power
(conservative estimate)

20,000,000
bits/sec

40
bits/sec

Try *really* hard to 'outthink' or 'out-intention' a supercomputer with a pocket calculator, or rewrite, delete, and edit the programs of the supercomputer to better serve you?

I chose the latter, and it made all the difference in my world.

Three years prior to connecting with 'My Guy on the 9th Floor' was the first time I was introduced to psychological kinesiology, or muscle testing, as part of a biofeedback toolset that I used to gain insight into what the heck was going on in my internal space.

But it was my daughter who was the catalyst that brought the practice directly into my field of awareness and began accelerating my internal journey.

Probably like some of us, my wife and I wouldn't say that we 'fought' but we 'energetically disagreed' or liked to have 'impassioned semantical discussions', but really, we were fighting. We were in denial of it at the time, just smushing those feelings down and running outdated programs ("She never listens to me or hears what I am saying." "He always needs to get a word in edgewise.") and reinforcing them in our subconscious supercomputers, but the (dis)ease we were creating began to manifest in our daughter.

Any time she would get a blemish, pimple, or itch, she would scratch it. On her face, arms, legs—anywhere there was a sensation, she would scratch until it was raw and bleeding. A lot of the time this would happen subconsciously, or at night, and she wouldn't consciously be aware of where the marks came from.

She began wearing band-aids to bed and to school to prevent her from picking and to cover her wounds.

Luckily, or serendipitously, a family friend was seeing a 'western medicine' General Practitioner (GP) at the time who also practiced psychological kinesiology as an ancillary to his western training. Over his fifty years of GP experience, he had seen too many patients whose symptoms and negative experiences were not helped through strictly western means, and he also saw remarkable progress, symptomatic improvements, and 'curing' in his patients as soon as he started integrating what may still be considered 'alternative medicine.'

In the first appointment, using muscle testing, the doctor was able to help our daughter uncover the reason she was picking her skin within seven minutes. It was us. When my wife and I argued, our daughter felt anxious, and her expression of that anxiety was to pick her skin.

Her picking was our family's 'canary in the coal mine' that there was (dis)ease among us. Talk about a gut-check moment. The petty bickering that we dismissed as 'well, that's just what couples do' was having a direct and physical impact on our daughter.

As soon as she was able to realize the underlying cause of her 'symptoms' and release the feelings she was experiencing that were causing the subconscious mind to sound an 'emergency warning' (in this instance the symptom of picking at blemishes), the 'compulsion' disappeared. That was it. Seven minutes with this amazing doctor.

Kids are closer to the source, but each and every one of us is an amazingly resilient, insightful, intelligent, expansive, and brilliant energetic being.

All of us have everything we need on the inside, and our energetic-selves are just waiting patiently for a stronger connection or a reconnection. But for many of us there is layer upon layer of conditioning and subconscious programing that keep us enmeshed with our three-dimensional experiences and apart from our energetic center.

It was the first of many 'reality' shaking insights and emotional, eye-opening experiences on our own journeys that slowly but surely led my wife and me toward greater happiness and peace and love, both for ourselves individually and within our relationship together.

Our process, however, took a bit more than just one seven-minute session. Possibly because we each had decades more worth of negative subconscious programs and patterns to identify and rewrite or overwrite, possibly because everyone's collection of 'expressions of reality' is so specific to their own experiences. We are all playing our own version of the first-person video game.

We continued to see this doctor together as a couple, and individually, for the next few months. Then the same family friend who had found such success on her way back to health with the help of this doctor, decided to get trained in a similar modality, and I happened to be the lucky recipient of her practice training.

My wife, whose background is in psychology and marriage and family therapy, followed soon after and expanded her range of tools beyond psychological kinesiology to include emotional and energetic clearing/healing practices.

I dove deep. To any subconscious technique, balance, or emotional/energetic process that came my way I said yes. I was ready, and I wanted more. More clarity, more internal distance between what I was coming to perceive as my 'real-self', and my emotions, thoughts, and reactions. More and more, I started to experience my three-dimensional world from a place of internal 'feeling', as opposed to 'thinking' and being 'stuck' in my mind. I began to tune in to my energetic systems much more clearly and be able to sense when something felt 'aligned' or 'not aligned' with my energy and vibration. I learned how to self-muscle test, so I could explore my internal space on my own, and clear any negative feedback loops, energy, and emotions much more quickly.

The more 'junk' I cleaned out of my subconscious mind, the quieter my mind became, the more easily I was able to discern what was 'real' *(for example: "Oh crap, that's a mountain lion. Make myself bigger and make a lot of noise!")* and what was just a programmed response or conditioned reaction *("That prospective client hasn't returned my email; it must be because I am not good enough and I don't really know what I am doing").*

The more I was able to become the Observer of my three-dimensional experiences *from my expanding fourth-dimensional perspective*, the more clearly the distinction between the two spaces came into focus.

There are many modalities to create more internal space on your journey to establishing or expanding your own fourth-dimension. Reiki, craniosacral therapy, resonance healing, medical intuitive sessions, PSYCH-K®, The Emotion Code, The Wim Hof Method, meditation, plant medicine, and biofield harmonics are just a few.

Experiencing a biofield harmonics session was the catalyst that connected me to My Guy on the 9th Floor. But the journey that brought me to that point was the primer of my system. So when I did experience a biofield harmonics healing session, my system was dialed-in and ready to experience some massive expansion and profound connection.

The two modalities that accelerated my personal journey are PSYCH-K® and The Emotion Code/Body Code. Both use muscle testing to tune in to the body's natural biofeedback system to guide you to areas ripe for expansion or cleaning out energetic junk.

Let's look at PSYCH-K® first. Created by Rob Williams, PSYCH-K® is:

- A non-invasive, interactive process of change with a proven record of success for over twenty-five years.

- A simple, yet powerful process to change subconscious beliefs that are self-limiting and self-sabotaging.

- A unique blend of various tools for change, some contemporary and some ancient, derived from contemporary neuroscience research, as well as ancient mind/body wisdom.

- A process that transcends the standard methods of visualization, affirmations, willpower, and positive thinking especially effective in the areas of behavioral/habit change, wellness, and stress reduction.

A number of different processes and energy balances within PSYCH-K® can be used to change unneeded or unwanted subconscious programs and reprogram self-limiting beliefs and self-sabotaging behaviors. It is also a great tool to expand your capacity to experience contrast and release resistance to that contrast internally. There is a treasure trove of positive personal insights and experiences to be gained through PSYCH-K® that are applicable in our personal and professional lives, and can bring a greater sense of purpose and satisfaction in all ways: professionally, through relationships, mentally, emotionally, physically, and spiritually.

The second, created by Dr. Bradley Nelson, is the Body Code/ Emotion Code. The Body Code and Emotion Code are diagnostic and insight "healing" tool sets that can be used to clear emotions and energies that create physical discomfort, emotional stress, and even eventual (dis)ease in the body and mind. The practice helps to uncover and identify trapped or hidden emotions, and even emotional resonances (the energy signature that remains after an emotion is experienced), as well as emotional traumas that can present themselves as mental, emotional, physical, and spiritual symptoms.

If anything in this book has resonated with you, I hope it is this section, because this is one of the most important areas to consider making an investment in for yourself, your family, and the world.

Explore different energetic/healing modalities, find one that works for you, ask for practitioner recommendations in your area, and start clearing out your own junk to help expand your capacity for fourth-dimensional observation and to live a more fulfilled life.

From personal experience, both modalities are absolute powerhouses and amazingly beneficial. The way I have employed them in my life is twofold.

I utilized the Body Code and Emotion Code to do some 'deep cleaning' of my body and mind. Instead of emotions and reactions 'happening' I began to be able to feel when there was something 'off' in my internal systems and consciously address the issue. Instead of being drawn back into feeling subjective to the visceral experience of those internal emotional 'drive-bys', I began to more easily release resistance to contrasts in my experiences and move into the role of the objective Observer of my three-dimensional world.

Using PSYCH-K® techniques, I was able to accelerate and better align my three-dimensional goals (business growth, prosperity, peaceful presence), energetically optimizing and aligning myself with concepts like the law of attraction. PSYCH-K® also helped me to expand my capacity to experience contrast and release resistance to that contrast internally, as well as tap into the brilliant bio-machine that is the collection of our three-dimensional receptors to unlock and uncover answers to questions I wasn't even aware needed answering!

Answers like where I needed to put my attention based on my goals, what I needed to let go of in order to experience more peace, and messages that my conscious mind couldn't access on its own but that my energetic-body and our collective intelligence had the answers to, ready and waiting.

Using these modalities in concert with each other, as complementary toolsets, has yielded and continues to yield exponentially expansive results. Did I ever fall back into three-dimensional patterns of negative reactions, thoughts, feelings, and emotions? Of course I did, and still occasionally do. I am human after all, like all of us. But, I began to be able to recognize what I was experiencing for what it was and became aware of how I was behaving in the moment much more quickly, shortening the time between my reactions to contrast and the release of resistance to that contrast. I began to be able to shorten the time between 'being had' by reactions, thoughts, feelings, and emotions and realizing that the only person that had anything to do with the way I was acting, feeling, and thinking was me. I began to 'observe' more than I reacted. And I slowly started to move from thinking, to feeling, to knowing, and toward becoming whole again.

PSYCH-K® is great for rewriting unneeded or damaging subconscious programs, aligning yourself much more strongly with the Laws of Attraction, instilling behavior and habit changes at the subconscious level, supercharging intention setting, and accelerating your alignment and actions toward achieving your 'rockets of desire.'

The Emotion Code and Body Code are great for 'clearing the internal runway' so that you can utilize the tools in PSYCH-K® more effectively and more readily expand your fourth-dimensional space. Links and resources are at myguyonthe9thfloor.com/resources.

Non-Acceptance Creates (dis)ease

Some things that affect us in life, we don't feel that we have control over until we gain distance from our three-dimensional experiences. We aren't *consciously* creating subconscious beliefs that end up working to our detriment, nor are we *consciously* storing negative emotions or energy away for a rainy day, you know, just in case we'll need them sometime.

These things are byproducts of being enmeshed with, and subjective to, our three-dimensional experiences. But resistance and non-acceptance are two areas where we can take conscious action to avoid creating more (dis)ease in our lives and in our world.

Experiencing contrast in thought, emotion, and feeling is amazing. It is what we are here for as energetic beings. But resistance to contrast or non-acceptance of things in our world that are out of our control, or that we don't necessarily align with can cause things to get backed up, reduce your vibrational frequency and, counter to any conscious intention or desire, accelerate you toward the things you don't want.

The more flexible your conscious mind can become, the more you can consider someone else's point of view or accept another's way of doing things, the happier you will be because you will be experiencing less resistance to the contrast in your life. The more distance you can put between your three-dimensional experiences and yourself as the inner-fourth-dimensional Observer, the more objective perspective you will gain *of* your three-dimensional experiences and the less power you will feel that they have over you. However, the more entrenched you are in non-acceptance and the more resistance you *choose* to experience, the more (dis)ease you will likely create for yourself.

(Dis)ease in your three-dimensional system can manifest mentally, emotionally, physically, and spiritually, and is caused by outdated subconscious programs, trapped negative energy or emotions, resistance, and non-acceptance.

It can manifest in relatively small ways, like negative thought patterns; low self-esteem or low self-worth; thinking ill of someone else; wishing to have what someone else has; being jealous, or resentful; or feeling stuck in grief.

And it can manifest in bigger ways. Depression, anxiety, PTSD, addictions, road rage, stage fright, sleep disorders, eating disorders, abuser/abusee vibrations, fears and phobias, victim/perpetrator frequencies, trouble losing weight, panic attacks, restless leg syndrome, susceptibility to viruses, and chronic pain or ailments are just a few symptomatic expressions of resistance, non-acceptance, trapped negative energy and emotions, as well as outdated subconscious beliefs running awry, all of which contribute to a lowering of your personal energetic and vibrational frequency.

This is where the connection between the body, senses, and conscious and subconscious minds becomes even more apparent because there is a good chance that if you are experiencing any of the multitudes of 'bigger' manifestations of (dis)ease, you are not even consciously aware that you are in resistance and non-acceptance, or that you are lowering your vibrational frequency.

We are making ourselves physically and mentally ill through resistance and non-acceptance because of our seemingly insurmountable entanglements with our three-dimensional experiences. The more we resist, the worse it becomes.

So how do we move *away* from (dis)ease and toward internal expansion, establishing ourselves as the Observer, and experiencing greater enjoyment in our lives? By looking at these three things: **quality of body, quality of mind, and living a fulfilled life.**

Quality of Body: Nourishment and Breath

"The truth reveals itself only to a healthy spirit in a healthy body."

— Paul-Henri Thiry

If you have ever spilled a sugary drink or soda on a computer keyboard, what happens? At best you have a fun new cleaning project on your hands, but you might be able to keep it working, albeit with a sticky key or two.

At worst the keyboard turns into a wrecked, unusable mess.

Because we are so enmeshed in our external experiences, we don't realize that the collection of our three-dimensional 'bio-machine' receptors (body, senses, conscious mind, subconscious mind) are *really* no different than any of the three-dimensional machines that we have created ourselves.

If a machine is misused, neglected, or actively set upon, it will have negative consequences. Too much strain on a car engine or transmission without proper maintenance, a corrupted hard drive, a soda-soaked keyboard, and a human body that hasn't been properly maintained through poor diet, not enough exercise, not enough hydration, living in resistance, or introduction of toxins and poisons, both energetic and physical, will all have the same outcome over a long enough timeline.

The machines will cease to work as intended.

Under mental, emotional, physical, and spiritual distress, our bio-machines begin to break down, even at the genetic level (genetic disorders and gene mutation). Remember everything is energy, and energy can neither be created nor destroyed, but it can change form.

High blood pressure, cardiovascular disease, cancers, and chronic illnesses with no obvious three-dimensional causes are all examples of energetic anomalies, mutations, or expressions that manifest themselves physically.

Going back to the car-and-driver analogy: The check-engine light is on, but because we are embodying the car, and not actively becoming the driver, we can't even see that a warning light is on, we can only experience the symptoms of (dis)ease that triggered the warning light in the first place. Even if we could intuit what the issue was, we would be looking at trying to find 'car' solutions, not 'driver' solutions. Again, it is a forest-for-the-trees issue. We are too close to the problem to even see it as the problem that it is.

So what can we do to give the physical components of our bio-machines the support, inputs, and care needed to optimize a high vibrational energetic system, and prime it for fourth-dimensional expansion? Here's the shortlist:

- **Eat as close to a whole-food, plant-based diet as possible.**

- **Get plenty of exercise and listen to your body.**

- **Get adequate, quality sleep.**

- **Hydrate, hydrate, hydrate.**

- **Breathe deeply, breathe vigorously, and (obviously?) breathe often.**

- **Balance, balance, balance.**

Now let's jump into each one.

Eat as Close to a Whole-Food, Plant-Based Diet as Possible.
Shop primarily in the fresh produce section of any grocery store
and prepare your own meals using ingredients that are as close to
nature as possible.

If you don't cook, learn how. This is a basic life skill that everyone
on Earth should at least have some exposure to. And by 'cook' I
do not mean having the ability to take something out of a package
and nuke it in a microwave. Practice! Cultivate the knowledge of
ingredients and skills of preparation methods that will serve you
for your lifetime. You can also utilize preparing and cooking a meal
as a 'mindful meditation' to help you be more present in your life.
Chopping, dicing, breaking down produce, and preparing food
requires focus and presence of mind, otherwise it can be all too
easy to cut yourself, miss a step in a recipe, or forget to take your
dish out of the oven. The more present you are, the quieter your
mind is. The more focused on a task you are, like preparing and
cooking a healthy (and delicious) meal, the less energy is going
to the thoughts, emotions, or reactions that might otherwise be
competing for your attention.

Increase your consumption of raw or cleanly cooked (little to no
processed oil) vegetables, fruits, legumes, whole grains, nuts, and
seeds.

There is a ton of research and resources out there on the benefits
of increasing these types of food (when prepared correctly), as well

as delicious recipes and methods of preparation so you don't have to completely abandon the comfort foods we all love. Links and resources are at myguyonthe9thfloor.com/resources.

Reduce or Eliminate Your Consumption of Processed Foods. This means anything packaged or that has been processed through manufacturing and comes in a wrapper or box. At a *minimum* balance your consumption of processed calories with your whole-food, plant-based caloric energy consumption. Personally, we still have plenty of 'manufactured-but-healthy' foods in our house (chips, crackers, breads, pastas) but our volume of whole-food, plant-based caloric consumption is massive by comparison. Additionally, we read every label of packaged food and avoid any with ingredients that we consider problematic as food additives.

This is the only car you get in this life. Read all labels of anything packaged or processed you are considering to consume so you know what types of fuel you are putting in your bad-ass bio-machine.

Don't recognize something on the label? Look it up. Educate yourself on the things that are being put into your processed, packaged, and manufactured food.

Avoid ingredients like 'natural flavor', 'artificial flavor', and 'natural identical' whenever possible. These cryptic umbrella terms are currently very loosely defined, and 'natural flavors' can actually include a variety of chemical additives. The FDA doesn't require companies to disclose what additional chemicals a particular 'natural flavor' contains as long as it is originally derived from plant or animal material. In addition to their original flavor source, these mixtures can contain more than 100 different chemicals, including preservatives, solvents, and other substances. These are defined as "incidental additives", and are not required to be declared on labeling.

Learn what has been banned for human consumption in the European Union versus what is still allowed to be put in processed, packaged, and manufactured food in the United States and North America, and vice versa. Give yourself the information so you can make the best choice for you.

Reduce or Eliminate Your Daily Refined Sugar Intake. Eliminate or drastically reduce *any and all* consumption of sugary beverages, candy, protein bars, energy bars, cookies, cakes, sweets, donuts, etc. This includes packaged/processed/bottled smoothies and juices, sweetened or flavored coffees and teas, sodas, and energy drinks.

As a society, we are over-sugared. It is in everything because it is addictive and food manufacturers want you to buy more of their products. If you need a smoothie or juice, make your own. Get a blender, a countertop bullet, or a juicing machine. Consume or repurpose (composting) all the great fiber and roughage that comes with your raw ingredients as well.

One reason managing sugar consumption in the US can be challenging is due to food labeling. Sugars are listed as grams instead of the more familiar teaspoon. If we do the conversion, around four grams equals one teaspoon. If we do the math, Coca-Cola has *sixteen teaspoons of sugar* in just one can of soda.

Personally, as a target to shoot for, we try to avoid any packaged or processed foods that have *any* added sugars, but as a practice we try not to buy anything that has over seven grams of sugar listed in the nutritional information (e.g. cereals, tomato sauce).

Reduce or Eliminate Your Animal-Based Protein Consumption. As a society, we are also 'over-proteined.' On average, most American adults eat about one hundred grams of protein per day, or roughly *twice* the recommended amount.[ix] Even on a vegan diet people can easily get sixty to eighty grams of protein throughout the day from foods like beans, potatoes, legumes, nuts, broccoli, and whole grains. In order to keep up with our species' animal protein demands, any number of steroids, antibiotics, and hormones as well as low-quality grain feed are given to 'animals for consumption' to get them onto the market as fast and with as much profit as possible. And those things pass through to us! Again, know what quality of fuel you are putting in your bio-machine.

Additionally, livestock is the world's largest user of land resources, with pasture and arable land dedicated to the production of feed representing almost 80 percent of the total agricultural land on Earth.[x] One-third of global arable land is used to grow feed, while 26 percent of the earth's ice-free terrestrial surface is used for grazing.[xi] Imagine the surplus of plant-based foods for human consumption that could be created if even the most ardent meat-eaters among us could reduce their animal-protein consumption to, say, three or four times per week? Behavior drives markets. If our behavior changes at scale, those market forces can help to bring our planet back into balance.

Unless you are humanely (and reverentially) killing an animal and utilizing every part of that animal for your family, please consider where the meat you are eating is coming from, and if you *really* need to be consuming as much as you do. Shop locally and look for humanely raised and slaughtered options whenever possible.

If you *are* killing and consuming an animal by yourself, consider how much is needed to sustain, or to thrive, for yourself and your family. Life and death are natural parts of our three-dimensional world, but ask yourself how much death and consumption is required *at our hands* for us to thrive individually and collectively.

Balance Your Healthy Fat, Healthy Carbohydrate, Naturally Occurring Sugar, and Protein Intake. Consume healthy fats, carbohydrates, sugars, and proteins using a balanced approach. This is a long-term benefit and sustainable approach to eating.

A Keto diet puts your body into ketosis or the metabolic process that occurs when the body begins to burn fat for energy because it does not have enough carbohydrates to burn. During this process, the liver produces chemicals called ketones. Following a Keto diet has been found to be a factor in developing a number of health risks, including nonalcoholic fatty liver disease (NFLD).[xii]

Keto diets, just like popular diets of the past (South Beach, Atkins), are short-term 'quick fixes' to three-dimensional 'problems', like a desire to lose weight. But that is just a symptom of an underlying or unaddressed energetic root-cause expressing itself physically. The reason an individual is overweight has nothing to do with overeating, sedentary lifestyles, or poor diets. Those behaviors are all three-dimensional symptoms of an underlying energetic (dis)ease in the bio-machine that is expressing itself in those symptomatic ways.

All any 'fad diet' or 'eating plan of the moment' really is, is a short term 'cure' for a three-dimensional symptom of an underlying energetic (dis)ease that we are not even aware of having.

Eating right for your blood type, following an Ayurvedic diet based on your Dosha, 8 Constitutions Medicine, and knowing your somatotype (ectomorph, mesomorph, or endomorph) are all great ways to gain insight into what the best balance of healthy fat, healthy carbohydrate, naturally occurring sugar, and protein is right for your very unique and specific biome.

Get Plenty of Exercise and Listen to Your Body. This one can't be overstated enough. Get moving. Start wherever you are on your journey and challenge yourself. Walking around the block, planting and tending to a garden, learning to dance, training for a marathon, making it through a CrossFit class without wanting to puke, learning to surf, taking a yoga class, making it to the top of a rock climbing wall—whatever your 'thing' is, look beyond your comfort zone and define what your challenge is, then go after it.

As soon as you achieve that first goal, look again beyond your own personal 'comfort zone horizon' and create another challenge for yourself. Make it fun. If you aren't having fun doing something, look for another physical activity that you enjoy or want to experience for the first time. Try a lot of different things until you find one (or a few) that resonate with you.

Keep at it. When you exercise, you are expanding your capacity to turn down the 'noise' of your subconscious mind. When you challenge yourself physically, you are putting yourself squarely in the present moment where all your intention and focus is going toward the experience at hand and, as a byproduct, creating more fourth-dimensional space inside.

Have you ever worked out, exercised, played a sport, or ran vigorously and felt great afterward? That is because the energetic-you is sitting on a lounge chair relaxing with a refreshing tropical drink in the internal space you are creating. There is no past (depression) or future (anxiety) because you have physically demanded that your bio-machine work hard in the present moment. And even if it is just for a moment, all the physical attention and exertion that you required of your bio-machine will have used up a lot of the energy that would otherwise go to your subconscious mind, figuratively 'starving' all the BS programs and software that usually run and that keep you enmeshed with your three-dimensional experiences.

Listening to your body is the other side of the coin. Part of expanding into your own personal fourth-dimension is more finely tuning your internal receptors so you can know when to push your bio-machine (body and mind) and when to rest your bio-machine. Tired? Get more rest and/or take some 'me' time. Sore? Take a rest day from strenuous activity. Mentally clouded, angry, anxious, or depressed? Get some exercise and clear your mind. Use diaphragmatic breathing exercises or meditation, or the 'burn it out' method to center yourself in the present moment. In pain? Realistically look at the pain and assess the cause. Was it something acute that you physically experienced (pulled muscle, rolled ankle, a broken bone, strained ligament or tendon)? Take the appropriate steps to diagnose and treat the acute physical pain.

In addition to western approaches (setting a broken bone, resting ligaments and tendons), this *includes* emotional and subconscious energetic work because when you raise your vibrational energy and clean out any negative or outdated programs, you are also improving the overall quality of your physical body, which can help you recover more effectively. Did the pain pop up seemingly out of nowhere, or has it been chronic, with or without a physical experience as the cause? If so it can easily be emotional, energetic, or due to resistance or non-acceptance. Look to one of the many energetic healing modalities/practitioners for assistance, just like you would a physical therapist, chiropractor, or acupuncturist for help recovering from an acute physical experience.

Get Adequate, Quality Sleep. The benefits of quality sleep are well-documented and numerous. It can help you:

- Get sick less often

- Stay at a healthy weight

- Lower your risk for serious health problems, like diabetes and heart disease

- Reduce stress and improve your mood

- Think more clearly and do better in school and at work

- Get along better with people

- Make good decisions and avoid injuries; for example, sleepy drivers cause thousands of car accidents every year

If you are having trouble sleeping, try making changes to your routine to get the sleep you need. You may want to:

- Change what you do during the day; for example, get your physical activity in the morning instead of at night, or vice versa.

- Create a comfortable sleep environment, and make sure your bedroom is dark and quiet.

- Set a bedtime routine and go to bed at the same time every night.

Take the needed steps for you, where you are, looking at the situation with radical honesty for yourself.

Too distracted? Remove all screens and electronics from your bedroom. Read an old-fashioned book if you need something to transition to sleep. Too restless? Get more exercise, and/or change the type, time, and level of exercise you are getting. Eating right before bed? Make sure to stop eating no less than three hours before going to sleep.

Have a sleep disorder? Sleep disorders can cause many different issues. Keep in mind that it's normal to have trouble sleeping every now and then. People with sleep disorders generally experience these problems on a regular basis. Common signs of sleep disorders include:

- Trouble falling or staying asleep

- Still feeling tired after a good night's rest

- Sleepiness during the day that makes it difficult to do everyday activities, like driving a car or concentrating at work

- Frequent loud snoring

- Pauses in breathing or gasping while sleeping

- Itchy feelings in your legs or arms at night that feel better when you move or massage the area

- Trouble moving your arms and legs when you wake up

Does that sound like you? Then enlist the help of an energetic healing modality and clean the junk out of your subconscious trunk for better sleep, better energy, and less 'internal chatter.'

Hydrate, Hydrate, Hydrate. Make sure you are getting the right amount of hydration for you. Some experts say a healthy person needs thirty to fifty ounces of water per day, some say about eight ounces of water for every ten pounds of body weight, and others say between half an ounce to one ounce of water for every pound that you weigh.

I have an easier solution. *Drink enough water so that you pee clear (or pale yellow) at least one time per day* at times when you are not consuming alcohol or caffeine, both of which are diuretics. Start with that simple goal.

The best way to achieve that goal is to always have water with you. If it's always in front of you, and you've always got water with you, it will be much easier to shift behavior to include drinking more water.

The benefits of adequate hydration include:

- Helping to maximize physical performance
- Having a major effect on energy levels and brain function
- Potentially helping to prevent and treat headaches
- Relieving constipation
- Helping to treat or avoid kidney stones
- Helping to lose weight
- Promoting cardiovascular health

**Breathe Deeply, Breathe Vigorously, and (Obviously?)
Breathe Often.** While breathing is a part of our autonomic
systems (our subconscious), who of us is ever taught to breathe?
It's a cryin' shame that we aren't. Watch a baby or child breathe.
Full expansive belly breaths. Have you ever seen a child sucking in
their gut? At some point along the way, the older we get, we move
away from our natural breathing rhythms.

There are many approaches to breathing that have been utilized
through time, from Buddhist meditation traditions to, more
contemporarily, the brilliant self-experiments of an amazing/
seemingly crazy (only at first glance though) Dutchman, Wim Hof.

The Wim Hof Method is a breathing and physical-stimulation
practice that heightens bodily oxygen levels by expelling more
carbon dioxide than it lets in.

Combined with cold therapy and mindset training, vigorous
breathing exercises such as the Wim Hof Method have been proven
to show improvements in:

- Stress reduction

- Faster recovery from physical exertion

- Better sleep

- Improved sports performance

- Enhanced creativity and more focus and mental clarity

The Wim Hof Method is also linked to reducing symptoms of diseases like rheumatoid arthritis, multiple sclerosis, Parkinson's disease, asthma, sarcoidosis, vasculitis, and several autoimmune diseases. Relaxed belly breathing, which we have already touched on in previous sections of this book, helps with centering yourself, relaxation, and clearing the mind. But both belly breathing and the Wim Hof Method are diaphragmatic breathing practices. Diaphragmatic breathing has a multitude of benefits:

- It helps you relax, lowering the harmful effects of the stress hormone cortisol on your body.

- It lowers your heart rate.

- It helps lower your blood pressure.

- It helps reduce the three-dimensional symptom of stress.

- It helps you cope with the three-dimensional symptoms of (PTSD).

- It improves your core muscle stability.

- It improves your body's ability to tolerate intense exercise.

- It lowers your chances of injuring or wearing out your muscles.

- It slows your rate of breathing so that it expends less energy.

Balance, Balance, Balance. Balance is not only one of the 'radicals' in the *Advanced Concepts and Challenging Thinking* section of this book, it is also one of the cornerstones of thriving in our three-dimensional experiences. It is only when things are off-balance in our bio-machines that we begin to experience (dis)ease that can manifest and present symptoms in any number of physical, mental, spiritual, or emotional ways.

Why? C'mon, guys, you know this one by now—because everything is energy.

Balance is paramount to success in our three-dimensional world as well as the *observation* of our three-dimensional experiences from our perspectives as the Observer.

Let yourself experience everything internally, then let all of those things go. Balance with yourself. Don't beat yourself up about it, whatever the 'it' is for you. Learn from it and grow. Balance with others. You have no idea what someone else is going through to cause them to act or behave in a certain way. This also has to do with radical empathy and radical acceptance. Remember, nothing anyone else does in your three-dimensional world has anything to do with the *energetic-you*.

The you who is (or is on your way to becoming) your own Observer is an energetic-you of balance, reflection, and being able to see both sides of any external experience, even if some of your bio-receptors might not 'agree with' or 'like' one side of whatever thought or idea you are entertaining.

The space that you are creating for the 'you-who-is-on-your-journey' to live a more fulfilled life and connect with your higher self (if that is your goal) is a space that is built on a foundation of balance, empathy, acceptance, and honesty with yourself and with every other person in your world.

This also means, sure, go ahead and have that cookie, or that slice of pizza, or that doughnut, or steak, or go ahead and buy the dress, or sweet hoodie, or a new game that's speaking to you, or whatever your 'thing' is. Just make sure that you aren't using anything in your three-dimensional experiences to cover up, silence, or ignore anything going on inside and balance whatever 'your thing' is with something opposite.

If it is junk food, have the treat, but continue to increase your whole-food, plant-based consumption and get exercise. If it is a game, or piece of clothing, or anything else material, go ahead and get it. Just balance it with volunteering for something that resonates with you, or donate gently worn or unused clothes and games to charity, whatever you want to do that helps other people. Alternatively, only buy your 'thing' when you need it instead of every time something new comes out (also reducing your carbon footprint); make sure your three-dimensional experiences are balanced.

And rest, for goodness sake. If you are exhausted, or sore, or need to recharge, listen to your body with empathy and take the time you need for yourself.

Stop chasing external 'things' for your happiness, or sense of self identity, or as a temporary alleviation of a deeper issue.

You are brilliantly, perfectly, and amazingly you! There is no one else who can be the energetic-you in our shared world in this time, place, and space. But anytime you look for satisfaction, happiness, or fulfillment *outside* of your inner space *first*, you are putting yourself out of balance.

Clean out the junk in your subconscious trunk, continue to expand your internal space as the Observer, take care of your bad-ass bio-machine and take the first step and the next step, and the one after that, on your journey inward and beyond.

Quality of Mind:
Expansion through Release

> *"The things you think about determine the quality of your mind. Your soul takes on the color of your thoughts."*
>
> *— Marcus Aurelius*

The Way You Speak and Think About It, That's the Way It's Going to Be

We create, co-create, enable-because-of-resistance, or need-to-experience-for-contrast everything in our three-dimensional world. From the most complex systems to the most personal experiences, that's it. Being able to look at our world through this 'focused' lens is part of radical acceptance and radical balance.

Whether your view of our world is one of heaven or hell on Earth, purgatory, as meaningless or meaningful, doomed or destined for salvation, scary or abundant, or any of the myriad perceptions in between, you will be right, because your personal perception energetically creates your personal reality.

We've spoken previously in this book about how you are *not* your thoughts, emotions, and reactions but you *are* implicitly *responsible for them* because no one else has any control over your thoughts, emotions, and reactions but you. It's up to you and only you.

If you speak, react, or think negatively, you are creating and/or allowing lower vibrational frequencies to emanate from you. You are putting out 'grand opening' signs to your world that your 'negative store' is open for business. And that is the exact business that you will attract!

If you are thinking, emoting, or saying things like, "I am not a nice person" or "I'm not good enough" or "I am unlovable" or

"OMG, I hate that person; they are so [enter adjective here]" or "Things will never be different than they are right now" or "Things were so much better before" or "I will never be happy" or "I will never find love", you are unintentionally creating, reinforcing, or attracting those negative things to you at the energetic level.

The way that we act and the things that we think, say, and express are the energetic building blocks of our three-dimensional world, positive or negative. Take a look at the *quality* of your mental landscape. What kind of internal world are you building? Is it positive, strong, resilient, caring, empathetic, accepting, and honest? Or do you find excuses, justifications, untruths, secrets, resentment, or negativity toward yourself or anything else in your life?

The quality of your mind equals the quality of your life. The rate of expansion you experience on your journey inward is directly correlated to your capacity for radical honesty, radical empathy, radical acceptance, and radical balance with yourself and with everything else in your experiences.

*Being Conscious and Experiencing Consciousness
are Two Different Things*

Consciousness is the *awareness* that you are a thinking, feeling being, and is the *practice* of observing your conscious life (your internal thoughts, feelings, and reactions as well as your external interactions) as you experience it.

However, if you feel like certain aspects of life are out of your control, or like you are 'stuck' in your experiences, it can be challenging to cultivate awareness of life as you are living it. Any time something happens that you are reactive to in action, thought, or feeling, it is like getting poked in a bruise. The reaction is immediate, and often of equal or greater force than the perceived offense.

The more aware you can be of your thoughts, feelings, and reactions instead of just 'having' them (or being had by them) the more you are moving into an expanded state of consciousness, and the less the bruise will hurt if it gets poked. You are effectively reducing the perceived impact three-dimensional experiences have on your mental landscape and on your energetic-self.

The more internal space you give yourself to challenge your own negative systemic 'beliefs' (the world is out of control, one political party or another is bad, there is evil everywhere, I am worthless, I am unlovable), and the more aware you become of the thoughts, emotions, and reactions as you experience them, the more you are moving toward embodying the Observer *of* your experiences instead of being the subject *in* the experiences.

Confused, Frustrated, or Fulfilled

There are only three states of mental being that you can have about anything in our world: confused, frustrated, or fulfilled.

Confused. There is something that you don't understand, are unsure of, or unfamiliar with.

Frustrated. There is something that you do understand and can comprehend, but are experiencing resistance to.

Fulfilled. There is something that you do understand and have either accepted and/or agree with it, or you have released resistance to it.

As you continue on your journey of internal expansion, you will begin to notice more and more fulfillment in your life and in your mind. The more systems of contrast and differing opinion or practice that you *release resistance to,* the less you will feel the perceived impact internally, as well as in your external world.

Just because something exists in the world doesn't mean it is going to pull you back into being a prisoner of resistance to that thing.

Begin to cultivate more internal awareness of your three-dimensional world, and you will begin to move more and more into experiences of fulfillment, and away from confusion and frustration.

The more you can be fulfilled in your mind, the more you will be fulfilled in your life. The more fulfilled you are in your life, the less resistance and unacceptance you will experience and the more expansion you will cultivate.

If You're in a Place of Darkness or Confused, Scared, Angry, Depressed, Anxious, Questioning, Whatever . . . Look for the Light. There Will Always Be a Light.

Sometimes literally, most times not. It will express itself in ways both explicitly individually and personally meaningful to you.

Everything except the 'good' in life—love, acceptance, gratitude, compassion, empathy—is either part of a three-dimensional system of contrast, created or co-created by us in our three-dimensional entanglements, or caused by resistance.

The good is of us, our energetic-selves. Of our higher-selves, God, Jehovah, Source, Spirit—whatever construct or label you ascribe to 'it.' Anything negative, challenging, hard, or devastating is part of our three-dimensional experiences and is here for us to experience the contrast and to release resistance.

The more you align energetically with the negative, the more negativity you will experience. The more you align energetically with the positive, the more positivity you will experience. This is part of radical balance with yourself and for others.

The challenge is that we all too often are too enmeshed with, enamored with, or think we are controlled by 3-dimensional influences so much that the external noise can drown out our inner-knowing and connection to the good that is part of each and every one of us.

The capacity to create momentum to move from where you are to where you are going on your journey is only within you. Nothing external of your energetic-self or that is of our three-dimensional systems will ever have the capacity to enable lasting, long-term change in your three-dimensional experiences without that change beginning within you at the energetic level.

One of my own examples of 'the light', in retrospect, came for a long time in the form of music. For about a year before I connected with My Guy on the 9th Floor, I would wake up almost every day with a song in my head. It became comical. Pretty much every day I would ask my wife over breakfast, "Hey, guess what song I woke up with in my head?" and she would look at me smiling, but with a 'Really? Are you kidding me? Again?' look on her face.

Because I wasn't as 'present of mind' or fully embodying my Observer at the time, I didn't have the awareness of what, in retrospect, was *really* happening. We would chuckle about it, and I would go on with my day.

Fast forward to two days after me and 'My Guy's' life-changing connection. I had committed to helping my dad move some things from their place to storage, and I woke up that morning with some of the old 'symptoms' that I had experienced for years.

Everyone has their own special blend of (dis)ease in their three-dimensional world, from mild to gnarly. In general, mine were pretty mild: a feeling of pressure in my chest with the inability to take a deep breath, having 'cloudy brain' or mental static, high blood pressure, and a general feeling of unsettledness (anxiety).

The day progressed, everything was moved to storage, and on my way home, still 'out of sorts' and experiencing my own special blend of (dis)ease that I knew all too well, a song popped into my head.

Now this example of 'light' is specific to my personal three-dimensional experiences, but this time, instead of dismissing it, and with my newly expanded fourth-dimensional Observer perspective, I asked, *"Is there a message for me in this song?"*

I pulled over and, using self-muscle testing, got a strong response.

Yes, there was a message for me in the song.

After pulling up the lyrics on my phone and, again using muscle testing, I found the line in the song that was the message. The line was *'Let me drive that [effing] train.'* I smiled, and then laughed out loud. Like I said, My Guy can be pretty hilarious.

I said, in my head and out loud, *"Okay, take the wheel,"* and I said it with all of the love and openness and acceptance that I felt in that moment. And then, ***schhhunk!*** We were synced up again. All the physical discomfort I was experiencing disappeared. Clarity, calmness, and a sense of 'peaceful presence' washed over me, and I felt good, *really* good, just like two days prior, and that's how it's mostly felt ever since.

In retrospect, I do wonder what the messages would have been if I was able to see my 'light' sooner, but the reality is I wasn't ready for it any sooner than exactly how I experienced it.

Your own 'light' can manifest in any number of myriad ways, and will most likely be personally specific to you. Increasing intuition, a new positive acquaintance popping into your life, similar messages or signs that keep popping up in different ways, music, something visual, something in nature (for example: you keep seeing dragonflies everywhere), or feeling 'drawn' toward something or someone are all examples of how the universe can deliver messages to you when you are open to receiving them.

Tend to the Garden on the Inside,
and the Garden on the Outside Will Grow

We are *in experiences* of our three-dimensional world, but we are not *of* our three-dimensional world.

Nothing—not other people, not money, not things, not medication in any form, not any experience in your external world—will bring you *lasting* happiness, joy, peace, abundance, or wealth unless you can first cultivate those things internally.

And the way to do that is through internal expansion and becoming a steward of your internal space.

You are the only one capable of becoming a steward of your internal space and creating a garden that flourishes. Only you are in control of your thoughts, feelings, and reactions even though you are not any of those things.

Emotions are there to be felt and can be used as signposts on your journey. Experience them all, feel them all, and let them all go. Negative emotions are amazing reflections of areas ripe for expansion and release and can be used as internal growth tools.

Ask yourself, *"Where in my body do I feel [the emotion]?"* Let yourself experience what the emotion feels like for you. Sit with it as you would sit with a good friend. In silence with relaxed belly breathing, or even in a quick five-minute meditation, ask yourself, *"Is there something I need to see, hear, or know? Is there something that requires action that I need to do?"*

Sometimes you can intuit an answer by looking at an emotion in this way on your own, and the emotion can release by itself by taking the time to reflect on it. Sometimes more time is required until further understanding is gained. If after some good effort with self-reflection you still feel 'stuck' in an emotion, enlist the help of an emotion code practitioner to clear the trapped emotional energy. The most important thing is not to push emotions down or suppress them. That is an all-too-common form of being in resistance and can lead to creating or co-creating (dis)ease in your system.

On your journey please remember, no one knows what anyone else is experiencing in their first-person video game. No one knows what anyone else is going through in their internal space, and everything is relative. One person's trauma or potentially deadly three-dimensional experience is another person's inconvenient bee sting. It is all relative to the experiencer.

Every one of us is playing *our own* version of that first-person video game, and a lot of people are still experiencing their reality as the car and not the driver. Be kind to everyone.

If you are a responsible steward of your *internal* space, then your *external, three-dimensional experiences* will benefit.
This is one of the upsides of radical balance. More peace, more freedom, more abundance, more love, more space, and an all-around better time in your world is all right there, waiting for you to tend to the garden on the inside. Release the negative or trapped energy, release resistance, release unacceptance, and watch your gardens grow.

Let Your Emotions be Your Compass as You Move from Thinking to Feeling to Knowing. As you are on your journey of emancipation from your entanglement with your three-dimensional world, you will begin to move from a state of *thinking* to states of *feeling* and *knowing*.

Being entangled with our three-dimensional experiences, our bio-machine receptors do a lot (okay, pretty much all) of the driving. We overthink everything when we behave as the 'car' instead of the 'driver of the car.'

Moving into your role as the Observer takes you from *thinking* toward *feeling*. How did that interaction with someone you disagree with *feel*? Start to tap into what your experiences feel like, instead of misinterpreting that the thought, reaction, or emotion is happening to you.

Be your Observer and question everything on your journey from thinking to feeling and knowing:

Where did that thought come from?

What lesson or message can I take from this experience?

How did that interaction feel? Do I want to repeat it, or can I make a change so a similar interaction in the future has a different outcome?

As you move more and more into a feeling/knowing state, you may start to observe greater contrast in your three-dimensional experiences. You might start to be more drawn toward experiences that *feel* good, and start to feel repelled from experiences that feel *not-good*.

At this point, it becomes less about releasing resistance, and more about listening to your intuition. This is moving from feeling to knowing. If you feel a situation or experience isn't right for you, enact change in your three-dimensional world *to* make it right for you.

Extract yourself from a negative situation, move toward experiences that are more aligned with your energetic self, or change the way that you are being (what vibration and resonance are you creating with your energy?) in an experience. A classic example of this that can be challenging for us is family gatherings, like holidays.

Say you don't get along with—or have a hard time being around—your family, but there is a family event coming up you feel you 'have' to attend. You have choices and you have options, regardless of how it might 'feel' to the contrary.

Think about your options, experiencing the feelings of contrast for each one internally, releasing resistance to each option, and then choose your path. Remember, stagnation is an illusion. You are always moving toward something, but whether you are moving toward something desirable or undesirable is entirely up to you.

So, in this example you can:

- Not go, and simply avoid the event altogether. But you have to be honest with yourself and others about why you aren't going, otherwise, you can easily backslide into feeling like you are being controlled by your three-dimensional experiences.

- Go, and communicate with love, empathy, compassion, and understanding the reasons why family gatherings are difficult for you. This is an opportunity for your vibrations of expansive influence to be experienced by others in your field. Open a potentially challenging or expansive (it all depends on your internal perspective) conversation, and enable others the opportunity to *(kindly)* experience contrast and have the opportunity to grow as well.

- Go, but don't say anything and let the 'status quo' remain. If this is your path, maintain the internal space between yourself and your thoughts and feelings, as well as anyone else's influence, as the Observer. Do not let yourself get drawn into being enmeshed with anything 'negative' in your three-dimensional experiences because nothing anyone else does, says, thinks, emotes, or reacts to has anything to do with you.

Whatever your scenario is, *think* about your options, let yourself *feel* the contrast of each option internally, and *release resistance* to any contrast to which you feel a mental, physical, spiritual, or emotional reaction. Then go with the option that you *know* is the best for the energetic-you *as the Observer* of your three-dimensional world.

The more you can regularly tap into your *feeling* and cultivate your *knowing*, or intuition, as the Observer of your experiences, the easier remaining in that state of knowing will be for you.

The Only Thing Constant is Change, and Internal Change Does Affect Your Outer World

Change is a major theme of the journey toward living a more fulfilled life and cultivating a stronger connection to your interpretation of higher self, higher consciousness, God, Source, Spirit, whatever your label is.

As you begin to change at the energetic level, the vibrations and frequencies that you resonate into your world are changing as well. These can have profound, and sometimes unintended, consequences in your life.

You may feel distance or alienation from certain friends or groups you were once close to. You may grow closer to, or be more energetically drawn toward, different friends or family members. As your capacity to safely experience and release resistance to contrast in your internal space grows, you will most likely encounter new people or groups in your life that you are newly resonate with and are drawn to. These visible changes in your personal resonance and vibration are reflective of the changes you are making at the energetic level, are byproducts of the expansion and energetic shifts taking place internally, and are natural. Your energy is changing, your vibrational resonance is changing, and you are actively changing the quality of your three-dimensional experiences through the changes taking place internally.

Your journey toward becoming the Observer of your world and beyond is inherently an internal journey. Conversely to how that might be perceived, it is not a journey of isolation or being alone. Quite the contrary. The journey inward is a journey of unity, support, connection, expansion, and abundance because the energy that you are cultivating is the energy of compassion, empathy, love, and acceptance for yourself and everything else in your three-dimensional experiences. Vibration and resonance are the byproducts of energy, and like attracts like.

Higher vibrations and resonance from abundant, positive, expansive *internal* energy attracts the same in your three-dimensional experiences. This is the source where concepts like the laws of attraction and abundance originate. It is all energetic.

Moving from 'Being Conscious' to Consciousness Leads to a Higher Consciousness. The Journey is the Goal

The more aware you become of your three-dimensional experiences as the Observer and the more you release resistance to contrast in your life, the higher you are raising your energetic vibration, and the more you are expanding your consciousness.

If you have gotten this far into the book and are still looking for an endpoint, or resolution, to it all, I have some bad news. This is not a journey with any kind of final destination, at least not as far as I can tell.

As of a few months after my forty-first birthday, in one afternoon, I had completely assimilated with my perception of my higher self. It took over forty years of curiosity and openness, and slowly moving away from thinking toward feeling and knowing. But it was the last three of those years that consisted of regular periods of intense self-reflection, self-examination, self-awareness, radical honesty, and growing my fourth-dimensional space that accelerated my journey of expansion.

When I first connected with 'My Guy', I thought, *"This is it. This is the meaning of life. This is the golden ring. I did it!"* But over the next few weeks, as the initial feelings settled, I began experiencing my 'new normal.' The initial elation and surprise subsided and I slowly came to realize this life-altering connection that I made to my higher-self was just a beginning.

It was the tiniest of particle-wave excitations in an even bigger energetic field that I had barely scratched the surface of. But I wasn't sad, or disheartened, or discouraged by this realization. I was energized. There is so much more to be discovered than what we can experience with just our bio-machine receptors. But the only way for us to discover it is to first journey internally.

Experience Everything, Let Go of Everything

Part of radical acceptance, radical balance, radical honesty, and radical empathy is allowing yourself to experience everything internally, and then *releasing* resistance to everything you just allowed yourself to experience. The more you cling to, covet, obsess over, or worry about *anything*, the more (dis)ease you are creating in your bio-machine: your senses, your body, and your conscious and subconscious minds.

Part of the way to create and expand your own internal space of observation is to let go of your three-dimensional attachment to everything. Does that mean you stop *caring* about everything? Absolutely not. Just because you release attachment to, or identification with, three-dimensional things does not diminish your capacity for love, understanding, compassion, empathy, or acceptance. It actually increases it.

For exercise, my thing is surfing. I love it and have been riding waves since I was young. It is one of the most physically demanding and holistically rewarding things that I have ever experienced: mind, body, and spirit.

Let's say I have a bad session and can't even catch a wave, or ding my board, or a car runs over my board in the parking lot. Am I letting any of those things ruin my day? Do I stop surfing because of a few bad experiences? No way. I let myself experience the frustration of not catching any waves or dinging my board or the anger and resentment that might flare up by having my board run over, but then I let. Them. All. Go.

Holding on to any of those feelings isn't going to rewind time and make me catch a wave, or not ding my board, or not have it be run over. So many things had to conspire to create the situation for any of those examples to occur, so I am not going to dwell on the past or on things I might perceive as being out of my control. The only way forward is to let it go and move on. Move through the experiences, release resistance to them, and continue on your journey.

That was a softball example. Let's look at a more challenging one: a sick child dying of an incurable affliction. If you are that child's parent, are you going to abandon them, stop caring about them, or not pursue every expert and treatment available to help your child just because you've released attachment to three-dimensional things? Of course not. But if you hold onto the grief, anger, resentment, frustration, hatred, sadness, and anguish that must be associated with that sick child's experience, you are not helping them, and you are not helping yourself. At. All.

Let yourself experience all of the emotions, thoughts, and reactions. But you need to let them all go as well, for your well-being and for the well-being of others.

Living a Fulfilled Life

> *"Don't await perfection... but be satisfied with even the smallest step forward, and regard the outcome as a small thing."*
>
> — *Marcus Aurelius*

This is the place where all the amazing internal work you have been doing to:

- realize you are not your thoughts, reactions, or emotions;

- accept that nothing anyone else does in our three-dimensional experiences has anything to do with you;

- move through thought, toward feeling and knowing;

- clear out any negative or trapped emotions and rewrite subconscious programs that no longer serve you;

- and expand your internal fourth-dimensional perspective to become the Observer of your three-dimensional experiences;

can start coming together in your three-dimensional world.

Now, this isn't to say that you haven't already begun to experience positive shifts in your life. I hope that you have. We *are* talking about quantum energy here, so the *instant* you make an energetic change, that shift begins to resonate throughout your world.

This place though, the place where you've started to assimilate all the aspects of expansive, energetic change we just listed, is the place in your journey when all the growth and expansion you have been cultivating can really begin to be felt in your experiences.

Also, please remember all of this is a practice. There is no magic pill or one-and-done approach to it. These practices are tools to carry with you on your journey.

Not 'Can I?', but 'How Can I?'

Think of something you want to do in your life because you are energetically drawn toward it, not something that has anything to do with outside influences.

Instead of asking yourself, *"Can I [insert your thing here]?"* ask yourself, *"How can I [insert your thing here]?"*.

'Can I?' is inherently a limiting and binary question. The answer is either yes or no. 'How can I?' is an expansive, creative, thought-provoking question that increases your neural plasticity and expands your capacity for arriving at creative, dynamic, and fulfilling answers.

Moving from Effort to Effectiveness

How can you use the internal, energetic shifts you are making to increase your positive three-dimensional impact? Stop thinking *more* work, and start thinking *what* works. 'Staying busy' and working long hours have too long been a benchmark for perceived 'success' in our external world, so much so that it is celebrated in certain cultures!

Inemuri, or the Japanese concept of being 'present while sleeping', is where an individual literally falls asleep during a commute or at work, in parks, in coffee shops, in bookstores, in shopping malls, or in any other public place. Now, going back to the *Quality of Body* section one more time, adequate sleep is paramount to a balanced bio-machine system. But in Japanese culture, not only are individuals who experience *Inemuri* culturally accepted, they are admired and respected because of their *perceived* effort or contribution. Literally falling asleep on the job may be a byproduct of great effort, but it is also a sign of ineffectiveness, and 100 percent a symptom of imbalance.

Microsoft Japan published the results[xiii] of an internal four-day workweek experiment from August 2019 and reported a 40 percent increase in productivity and a 23 percent decrease in energy consumption.

Perpetual Guardian, a New Zealand trust management company, announced a 20 percent gain in employee productivity and a 45 percent increase in employee work-life balance after a trial of paying people their full salary for working a four day week.[xiv] The company made the policy permanent in October 2018.

By starting with *'How can I . . .?'* and observing any situation from the perspective of opportunity-without-resistance (remember the family gathering example), you are equipping yourself with the internal tools to move toward greater effectiveness without the perceived need of a performance of effort.

Your Capacity for Positive Three-Dimensional Impact is a Direct Result of Your Positive Internal Growth

The more you observe, the more objective you can be with your world. The more objective you are with your world, the more space you create to pursue activities that are aligned with your elevating energy, frequency, and vibration, and the greater your capacity for positive impact beyond yourself becomes.

But, the work must start on the *inside* because you will never be able to out-perform your own self-image. Practicing radical acceptance, radical balance, radical honesty, and radical empathy begins with experiencing all of those things internally about yourself. The more accepting, balanced, honest, and empathetic you can be with yourself, the more capacity you will have to be those things with others.

The more you cultivate space between yourself as the Observer and the thoughts, reactions, and emotions that are part of your bio-machine, the more space you gain to expand and elevate your own self-image and self-perception. Become masterful at starving your doubts to death because a 'doubt' is just part of a three-dimensional construct of influence (getting messages of 'you'll never be good enough' when young), and not truly a part of the energetic-you.

You must begin to elevate yourself in order to elevate anyone else in your three-dimensional world.

Marry Your Talents With Your Interests, From the Inside Out

Talents are innate and everyone has them. We get caught up in our external world, and the outside influences of those experiences can mar the lens through which we view ourselves, but only if we let them.

Clean your lens and reconnect to your energetic self who is not enmeshed with the three-dimensional 'simulation' of your first-person video game. Take your focus off the simulation, start focusing on your interior space, and *that* is where you can reconnect with the imaginative-you, the expressive-you, the effective-you, and the inventive, energetic-you on your journey of reconnection and alignment. Allow yourself to rediscover what your very important and very personal talents are. Remember back to when you were young. What was something that came easily to you?

Mine, for as long as I can remember, has been visualization (being able to see things clearly in my mind) and distilling complex things down into more simple things. Even when I was little, I was able look at, say, directions for furniture assembly, and be able to see the steps completed in my mind.

That said, talents are rarely cultivated in a vacuum or strengthened in isolation. Would Ludwig van Beethoven have been as prolific as he was without being born into a musical family, or experiencing the harsh and intense training his father subjected him to at an early age? Would Michael Jordan have risen to the heights he did without being born into an athletic family, or being cut from his high school basketball team, or experiencing the intense competition with his siblings that he did?

Regardless if we interpret the influences in our lives as 'good or 'bad', or how extreme the impact of the contrasts we experience are, the families and situations we are born into are the perfect incubators for each and every one of us. Sometimes though, it does take time and perspective to recognize it.

A running contrast between me and my dad when I was younger centered around our differing approaches to problem solving, and it was a source of conflict between us for years. I would want to jump right into things, figure it out for myself, or skip steps in a process because to me, I could already see things coming together in my mind. But through the view from *his* video game, my dad's perspective was that the way to do something 'right' was based around systems, and if there was a process and procedure to follow, you followed it. From getting his MBA, to a supply chain officer during Viet Nam, and eventually as a finance executive in his career, this approach served him well throughout his life.

Even though I was resistant to his approach growing up, I was awash in the exposure to his way of doing things while my subconscious supercomputer was being built. And, as much as I revolted and resisted through adolescence and young adulthood, I was also subconsciously incorporating parts of 'his way' of doing things into my life.

Throughout my professional career as an designer I would use my 'natural talent' as well as the tools of systems and processes I learned from my father to develop successful, simplified solutions to detailed business requirements or complex project specifications. And I've continued to utilize this combination on my personal journey of expansion. Quietly 'working the problem' in the background of my mind while diving deeper into myself, so that when I connected with 'My Guy', I was primed to co-create this process-based, energetic 'user guide'.

Interests are things we enjoy and get good at. Marry your talent with something you enjoy and have gotten/are getting/or want to get good at.

Don't have a talent or interest, not good at anything? BS. We all have something that we are innately drawn toward or that makes us feel good in a positive way. Math, science, engineering, sports, the arts, writing, problem solving, helping people, being a parent, listening . . . whatever you have a natural proclivity toward or something that you are energetically drawn to, can become a talent. It is up to you to recognize it and cultivate it.

I discovered, or uncovered, my interest in design in first grade. I was doing homework at the dining room table, and had doodled some drawings on my folder and in the margins of my papers. Lines, shapes, scribbles, and abstract objects were scattered here and there, but it was two lines in particular that brought the power of design fully into my young field of awareness. In and amongst my random doodles, I had inadvertently drawn a swastika. I had no idea what it was at the time. To me, I was just drawing different lines and shapes but it was something all together different to my mother, and her reaction was swift and impactful when she came to check on how my homework was going.

"What did you do?? That's a swastika!", she hissed with exasperation and embarrassment, furiously erasing the doodle on my page. Finishing her removal of the offending lines, she trailed off, "If your father were to see that...", and went back into the other room.

There was no reprimand beyond that, but in this moment I was shaken awake to the power of design. *"How could two lines cause that serious of a reaction in my mom?"*, I thought, stunned by what had just happened.

I had to know more. At the time, our Wikipedia was the Encyclopedia Britannica, so I looked up what a swastika was. I learned that it was an ancient symbol that has been in human culture since at least 10,000 BCE. I learned that it has held different meanings throughout the ages, from the 'good' (the modern derivation of the word *swasktik* comes from sanskrit and means "conducive to well-being.") to the 'bad' (the Nazi movement co-opted and corrupted the symbol so completely that it has come to be associated with hatred and skin-color bias in contemporary times).

I was shocked and in awe. How could something as simple as two lines carry *so* much meaning for *thousands of years*, regardless if it was labeled or interpreted as 'good' or 'bad'? This was the beginning of my fascination with design, and how impactful the meaning and messaging that we derive from symbols, shapes, and language can be.

By seventh grade, I knew definitively that I wanted to be a designer when I grew up, and I wanted to use the power of design to change the world for the better. I took every art class I could and, as my interest in design and the refinement of my skills grew, I was able to incorporate my 'talent' for breaking down complex systems into simpler concepts with my 'interest' for design.

By marrying my talent with my interest, I was able to cultivate a successful and fulfilling career in the design field, as well as expand my capacity for impact beyond myself by using that marriage to support the work of non-profit groups and environmental initiatives that resonated with me.

A Journey of Continual Expansion

Expansion of Thought, Expansion of Your Capacity for Action, Expansion of the Capacity for Impact Beyond Yourself. When you expand beyond your thoughts, emotions, and reactions, you are simultaneously expanding your capacity for positive action.

The more radically honest you can be with yourself, the more honestly, empathetically, balanced, and with-acceptance you can live your three-dimensional life with others. You will begin to feel what is right for you and you will become more aware of opportunities for action in your own life.

Seek out experiences that help you deepen your understanding of yourself. Challenge yourself. Find the edge of your comfort zone (safely) and explore it: mentally, physically, emotionally, and spiritually.

Identify experiences that make you feel good, and that are aligned with your energetic-self that you would enjoy doing for 'work.' Cultivate your talents and interests toward where you want to go professionally and personally. That said, you may not always have your ideal experience and the way you earn a living line up exactly. This is part of experiencing contrast and radical acceptance.

As soon as I was old enough to work, I took a job at a rotisserie chicken place that was within walking distance from my parents' house. I recognized that in order to survive and eventually thrive in the systems that we have all agreed to experience, money was a requirement.

I worked that job through high school and the experience allowed me to have money for gas and the space for other activities that were more fulfilling to me, like surfing. There were definite experiences of contrast in this job. From dishwasher to delivery driver, to cleanup and prep, rodding marinated chickens in the cold walk-in, and cleaning the hot, greasy rotisserie each night. I was awash in new experiences and new contrasts.

During college and beyond, I continued to work in restaurants in a number of 'front of the house' roles: as a busser, back-waiter, food runner, bartender, and server. Did I love these jobs and were they fulfilling? Not always, but I found ways to be present and enjoy the moments within the work that did fulfill me in different ways on my journey. The people I worked with who became lifelong friends, the relationships with regular customers, and experiencing the highs and lows of being in the weeds during a slammed shift or slogging through a slow season were all extremely contrasting and expansive experiences to have. My wife and I even met each other while working in restaurants.

Were these jobs hard work and demanding? Absolutely, but I moved through the experiences of these different positions because these jobs continued to fit well with *my own* first-person video game at that time, and in that place. These jobs also acted as a financial buffer as I cultivated new experiences following my passion for design as a profession, and when my wife and I welcomed our daughter into our world. But these are my experiences, and this was my path.

The important thing to take away is that you may not always be doing what you love or are passionate about in order to cultivate monetary income, and it may take time to cultivate your talents and interests. But being present and allowing yourself to experience the contrast in any situation without resistance gives you the opportunity to grow your capacity for acceptance, empathy, balance, and honesty with yourself and others.

Everything you do or every 'job' that you work is an opportunity to experience and release resistance to contrast in your life and treat each opportunity as a signpost on your journey.

Start doing positive, uplifting things that you enjoy (elevate your vibrational resonance). Challenge yourself (stagnation is an illusion and unacceptance creates (dis)ease), clean the junk out of the trunk (emotional and energetic healing; again, this one is huge), eat better for you, and start living an authentic life (from the inside out, not the outside in) on your journey toward fulfillment and beyond.

Section V

Advanced Concepts and Challenging Thinking: Moving Through the Radicals

"The more radically you can change your thinking, the more radically you can change your life."

— Bryant McGill

Connecting to Your Own 'Guy on the 9th Floor'

The whole journey of moving toward *your own expression* of your higher-self or higher-consciousness is a journey of moving *through* thoughts, emotions, feelings, and contrast. Another way to think about it is that it is a journey of allowing thoughts, emotions, feelings, and contrast to move *through* you.

Whichever way you choose to perceive it, the result of the journey inward is the same:

- an expanded capacity to experience contrasts in your three-dimensional world without attachment,

- an expanded capacity to release resistance to your thoughts, emotions, feelings, and three-dimensional contrasts, and

- an increased capacity for growth by allowing yourself to experience radical balance, acceptance, honesty, and empathy internally.

Remember this is a process and practice of inward and then outward growth and expansion.

The radicals, in retrospect, were a thought-exercise process on my journey that I *needed* to move through on my path to connecting with my higher-self. I can't say that you will need to move through these radical concepts on your own journey, but I do think it might be part of all of our paths inward and beyond.

This is because the only way that I personally know to grow into the space beyond our three-dimensional world is to increase the capacity for personal, internal expansion; first through thought, and then through feeling.

There is one important thing to consider before jumping into this section of the book. The radicals are a package deal. You can't have radical honesty without radical empathy, otherwise, you can easily start living life like a jerk. You can't have radical acceptance without radical balance because if you aren't being 100 percent balanced with yourself, or are still fostering resistance to the contrasts you experience, it can be challenging to even accept *yourself* sometimes, let alone anyone else.

You have to entertain the concepts of radical honesty, balance, empathy, and acceptance all together because they are interdependent concepts of expansion. They support, build off of, and enhance the expansion of each other. However, the radicals don't necessarily have to be experienced all at the *same time*.

I hope most events in your life *aren't* opportunities to experience the radical's 'superfecta', if you will, because situations that encompass all the radicals tend to be much more drastic in their contrast and impact. But, the more you challenge yourself with these concepts in your internal space, the more you push your threshold of what you are willing to let yourself consider, experience, and release resistance to *internally*, the more you will begin to see how they fit together and are naturally interdependent concepts.

Now, these radicals may not be easy 'membranes' or 'veils' of thought for everyone to move through. On the spectrum of contrast available to think about in the vast collection of human knowledge and experience as we know it, there are a multitude of amazingly positive, beautiful, uplifting, wonderful, tragic, horrific, disgusting, and terrifying things to entertain. The challenge of moving through your own radicals is to let yourself think about, experience internally, and release resistance to completely as many instances on both sides of the spectrum as you are ready for, or are willing to let yourself consider.

That's it. There is no magic, no test, no 'five questions to cross the Bridge of Death', just you thinking about the most uplifting and most gnarly things you can possibly imagine, experiencing the feelings of each thought internally, releasing the thoughts *as well as resistance to the thoughts*, and in the process accelerating your capacity for expansion. This exercise in radicals can be unnerving, challenging, triggering, or traumatic if you are holding onto resistance in any way, especially once you start to get into the 'deeper water' areas of thought.

Remember, only you are in charge of your internal space and only you know where you are on your journey. The journey to a fulfilled life, or your higher self or higher consciousness is primarily a self-guided one, so take your time and go at your own pace. Slow down and let go *(of all of it)* in order to accelerate your internal growth.

Whenever you are ready to push the envelope of the thoughts, emotions, and contrasts within your bio-machine as the Observer, this section of the book will be here.

Potential trigger warning: If you are in a state of heightened resistance (or resistance of any kind) or are experiencing any kind of energetic resonance of a traumatic experience, please consider connecting with an energetic healer, a holistic health practitioner, medical intuitive, PSYCH-K® facilitator, or Emotion Code Practitioner before jumping into this section of the book.

Clearing or resolving any resistance, trapped or hidden energy/emotions, or negative/outdated subconscious programs/software is very important before you embark on the more radical thought exercises in this book.

Radical Energy

Throughout this book, we have looked at how everything (ourselves; everything in our three-dimensional world; everything beyond our three-dimensional experiences and Observer perceptions), *absolutely everything*, is energetic by nature.

Energy is what all things are made of, including things we can't perceive, might be considered intangible (thoughts, feelings, emotions), or don't have the capacity or tools to experience just yet (other expressions of existence, different dimensions of experience).

Because of its nature, all energy has vibration and resonance. All 'matter' is a form of observable energy that is in one state of potential or another. And energy is the very connecting 'fabric' of *everything* that ever has, is, or *will* be because of the substrate of quantum fields and connection points of quantum entanglement that energy moves through. None of which are subjective to our collective perceptions of space, time, and dimensionality.

Things can exist in multiple dimensions because of quantum fields and states of potential (the substrate that energy flows through), and everything is connected because everything is energy (connects to all things in all dimensions because energy is also quantum).

Because of all that, our concepts of time and space are not fixed and absolute, but *completely subjective* to our observational, experiential, and perceptive *capacity*.

And by expanding our *capacity*, we are expanding our energetic *potential* for greater connection to ourselves, our family, friends, community, and everyone and everything in our world and worlds beyond ours.

Everything, everywhere, in all dimensions at all times is happening simultaneously, right now. And now. And now (it's kind of a perpetual thing). This includes spirits, aliens, ancestral energy (and the ancestors too, actually), past lives, future lives, different versions of now, and higher dimensional beings.

We just don't all have the *internal* tools developed, or three-dimensional machines created, to perceive it yet. But just because we can't perceive something with our bio-machines doesn't mean it doesn't exist. This is where we, again, get into some big picture thinking because it challenges the foundation of many of the three-dimensional systems that we have created to make sense of our world and our place in it.

The only limitation you have to tap into the energy of the universe and connect to your higher self is you. Remember, this book has nothing to do with me, or with your three-dimensional experiences. This is about the *energetic-you* that is pure potential, light, love, compassion, empathy, joy, peace, abundance, and understanding, and is more than the sum of your three-dimensional parts.

The energetic you who is a creator of worlds and can experience fulfillment, peace, abundance, and joy in your three-dimensional experiences here and now simply by expanding your perceptions of your world *internally*, expanding your capacity to experience contrast and release resistance to that contrast *internally*, and by allowing yourself to move through thoughts and emotions *without* resistance and *with* honesty, balance, empathy, and acceptance.

You have the energy of the universe, Spirit, Source, God, higher self, higher consciousness, enlightenment (whatever label you want to use) coursing and flowing through you, around you, and *making up you*, whether it is perceivable to you or not.

That is the radical nature of universal energy.

Radical Honesty

This is about radical honesty with yourself and others.

Only by cultivating an ever-growing space of radical honesty with yourself *internally*, will you begin to be more comfortable expressing kind and empathic honesty with others.

Radical honesty, as are all the radicals, is a *practice*. They are concepts that you are bringing into your field of awareness, allowing yourself to experience and release resistance to, and carrying with you on your journey as tools of expansion.

Now you might be in a place on your journey where you read these words, have already assimilated the concept of radical honesty in your life and are 'walking the walk.' If so, awesome; keep reading and see if there is any new information for you to experience.

Or this could be the first time you've ever considered the concept of radical honesty at all. If so, fantastic. Take it slow, continue to grow your internal space by honestly looking at your thoughts, reactions, and feelings, and differentiating if those three-dimensional things are coming from a place of love, gratitude, abundance, empathy and balance, or if they are coming from a place of resistance and negativity.

Trying is Lying, and Eradicate 'Can't' and 'Should'
from Your Vocabulary.

If you're "going to try" to do something, that means you are experiencing resistance to 'whatever the thing is that you're thinking about.'

"Ohhh, I'll *try* to make it to your party. . ." Nope. Either you can and do want to, or you don't want to. Be honest with yourself so you can be honest with others.

Think about a party, gathering, or event that is upcoming in your own life that you are feeling resistance to attending. Family reunion, Christmas dinner, Seder, Ramadan, frenemies' baby shower, company picnic, bachelor/bachelorette party . . . whatever first pops into your head.

Follow that 'resistance to whatever your thing is' as far as you can, being radically honest with yourself, down your thought trail about the source of the resistance until you can't go any further. Remember to look at where in your body you are feeling the resistance. Let yourself experience what the resistance feels like for you. Again, sit with it as you would sit with a good friend. In silence with relaxed belly breathing, or even in a quick five-minute meditation, ask yourself, *"Is there something I need to see, hear, or know? Is there something that requires action that I need to do?"*

By allowing the answer to come to you (moving from feeling to knowing), experiencing the answer with radical honesty *for yourself*, and letting any resistance to the 'core reason' to your aversion to the event go, you are strengthening your role as the Observer. You are also cultivating awareness of some of the deeper subconscious programs constantly influencing your three-dimensional life. High fives all around.

If you get stuck on your thought path and need help getting past a point of resistance, that is normal. Ask for it. Ask a trusted friend for some honest perspective, or connect with your energetic healer, holistic health practitioner, medical intuitive, PSYCH-K® facilitator, or Emotion Code Practitioner and clear the blockage or resistance you're experiencing so you can continue on your journey of internal expansion.

Words Like 'Can't' and 'Should' Distance You from Your Energetic Self, as Well as Others. Think about your life and something that you 'should' do. Starting to exercise, updating your resume, applying for the job you really want, learning how to cook . . . whatever a bigger 'should' is for you. When you have it, say to yourself, *"I should [your answer here]."*

Whatever your thing is, you are going to make an honest decision about it, right now in this moment. It's either yes or no. You either 'want to' or you 'don't want to' and there's another reason that accompanies the no.

It usually starts with 'because.' If you get a 'no-I-don't-want-to-because', follow the 'because' in your mind until you start getting real with yourself.

Say you follow that thought trail and end up at, "no I don't want to because I'm afraid." Keep going further if you can. Why am I afraid? What is underneath the fear? What pops into your mind? Remember, radical honesty with yourself. Follow the thoughts, peel back the layers of your conscious mind, and dig for a radically honest answer that resonates, that feels 'right', even if it might also feel uncomfortable in the moment.

If you feel resistance to something you experience internally, and *really* can't figure out the 'why' of the resistance, and the situation is still causing you distress or (dis)ease, then it is again time to look for assistance as you continue expanding into your fourth-dimensional Observer perspective.

Can't is another 'distancing' word. It disconnects you from an honest relationship with yourself and with anyone else. 'Can't' make it to an event or gathering? What is the reason behind the can't? If it's 'I don't want to', what is behind that? Why don't you want to? Remember radical honesty with yourself so you can be honest with others in your world. Keep peeling back the layers until you arrive at a radically honest answer that gives you 'truth bumps' - that depth-charge of an internal feeling when you feel the truth of something at your energetic core.

If your 'can't' is more personal, like, "I can't do it.", that can easily be an expression of self-limiting beliefs and self-sabotaging subconscious programming, and not a message that originated from the energetic-you. Whose voice are you hearing just behind statements like "I can't do it."? Is it your voice, or could it be that voice is really of your father, or mother, or grandparent, or any other indelible relationship in your experiences?

Cultivate greater awareness and recognition of the everyday language that we all use that can actually be attracting us to the things we don't want in life.

Examine self-limiting, self-sabotaging, and self-defeating speech and thought. Are those words and thoughts coming from a place of empathetic honesty for yourself? Or is it just another of the conditioned programs of (dis)ease that we have all experienced in our lives?

Radical Acceptance

Simply put, radical acceptance is a thought exercise where you, as your own Observer, can accept everything in our three-dimensional world exactly as it is. The good, the bad, the ugly, the beautiful, the destructive, the miraculous, the evil, the benevolent, the offensive, the illuminating, the hateful, the loving—all of it.

Only when you can radically accept **everything** *exactly as it* is in your three-dimensional experiences, will you truly be able to shake off the last vestiges of three-dimensional imprisonment that pretty much all of us have experienced or are experiencing.

Now, does acceptance mean non-action in your three-dimensional experiences? Not in any way, shape, or form. If you are inspired or drawn to take action against what you perceive as injustices in our world, do so. It is your journey. But make sure you are doing so from a place of peace, centeredness, and compassion.

Because if you are taking action against something you consider 'evil' (say as a women's rights advocate, or as a victim's advocate, or to end rape culture or radical extremism, or to dismantle the institutionalized racism still present in many three-dimensional systems) *with resistance* to the thing you are trying to take action against, you are energetically and vibrationally aligning with the very thing you are trying to fight.

Recent illustrations of this can be seen in the United States in clashes between anti-fascist and white supremacist groups, or predominantly black communities and militarized police forces.

Violence will always beget violence, and hate will only breed more hate if the energy that is used to combat the thing you are fighting is the very energetic signature *of* the thing you are fighting.

Workbook Download:

Please visit myguyonthe9thfloor.com/resources to download the printable workbook that accompanies the exercises in the Advanced Concepts section of this book.

An Exercise in Change and Acceptance

Change is the *only* constant. Accepting that in every form you could possibly imagine is part of radical acceptance. Go ahead and grab a piece of paper and a pencil, because we are going to make some lists.

Working from the fourth-dimensional space you've created, list ten changes that you can imagine that would be *negative* in life, and let yourself think about them as the Observer.

Stay in the present moment as well, but take each of those ten things and think about them one at a time. Think about them, let yourself experience them, and then release them. No dwelling, no clinging to, and releasing resistance to whatever you have written down as you go.

As soon as you sense an emotional, physical, mental or spiritual response, let yourself feel it, slightly distance yourself from it by letting yourself experience the *present moment* more strongly and then release it. Use real-life examples and use your imagination; let yourself get out there. Start small, but keep pushing the limit of what you are ready to let yourself experience and release as the Observer of your three-dimensional mind.

Here's a hypothetical example to get you started. You write down, 'Car accident: fender-bender, no injuries, but my fault.'

Let yourself feel that experience. The good and the bad (the accident sucks, but thank goodness no one was hurt. You could also look at it as a reminder to be more present and undistracted; look at all perspectives). This is also a big part of radical balance.

Are you angry with the other person or are you angry at yourself? Did you start beating yourself up about it, or did you immediately turn toward the other driver with hostility?

Regardless of which one it was, follow that thought and remember that nothing anyone else does in your three-dimensional experiences has anything to do with you. Don't take it personally.

Let yourself experience this hypothetical accident, and all the emotions and bodily responses associated with it and let them all go.

Move onto the next example you wrote down, and do the same thing. If you get stuck on a thought, write yourself a note or two about where you got stuck, and you can come back to exploring that particular example later.

Sometimes these thought exercises can trigger a deeper response than expected. If you can't get past a thought, or are experiencing a deeper reaction than expected, seek out assistance to help you get past your mental, emotional, physical, or reactive stuck point, clear any residual energy associated with the core situation you are reacting to, and continue on your journey of expansion into your own fourth-dimension.

Next, list ten changes that you can see that would be *great* for your life, and do the same thought exercise.

Again, start small, but push yourself. Imagining you can fly, and where'd you go and what you'd see (check out some drone footage on YouTube and let yourself feel the elation and exhilaration of soaring), or finding out you won $5,000 in a contest you don't even remember entering, getting a promotion, or being a rock star.

Let yourself experience the feelings associated with each scenario. Again, the good and the bad (if you can fly and soar through the sky, what would happen if your powers disappeared and you began to plummet toward the ground?). Let the emotions associated with each scenario flow through you, but do not hang on to them. Let yourself feel them, then let them go. This part is immensely important.

When emotions, thoughts, feelings, and subsequently, reactions are experienced, you have to let them go. Retaining negative emotions is poisoning us collectively, and affecting us at an energetic, vibrational level as individuals. We are seeing the symptoms of this (dis)ease everywhere.

Next, make another pair of lists. Ten more negative and ten more positive examples of changes that could occur in your three-dimensional world, thinking of the good and bad that could come out of each example you write down. Go as 'big' as you are comfortable going (asteroid impact, nuclear war, death of a loved one; or on the other side of the coin: peace on Earth, an end to world hunger, or having the-thing-you-love-to-do expand into an amazingly rewarding and lucrative career) and do the exercise again.

After this exercise, shift to getting in the habit of letting yourself experience and release the outcomes, both good and bad, of any scenario or thought that should pop into your mind as your own Observer, making sure to let the feelings go each time. These exercises in acceptance don't need to be long reflections or meditations. Have the thought, experience the feelings of the thought internally, and release resistance or attachment to the thought and the feelings.

Reminder: Letting go (releasing resistance) is the single most important part of this process of expansion.

Radical Empathy

At its core, radical empathy is about cultivating the ability to be able to see both sides of any and all possible three-dimensional experiences you can think of regardless of how in opposition, or 'in-resistance' you might feel. Remember, a big part of this journey is about releasing resistance to the contrasts in your life.

Consider it a radical game of 'put-yourself-in-their-shoes' that you only need to play by yourself on your internal journey. Here are some concepts from earlier in the book to give you a starting point and some perspective on your journey through radical empathy:

- We (and everyone else in the world) are not our thoughts, feelings, and reactions.

- The more resistance we cultivate to any of our experiences, the more (dis)ease we will create in our lives. Everything from a chronic sore neck to OCD, to jealousy and rage, and everything else on the negative energetic spectrum is a symptomatic expression of that (dis)ease.

- Everyone is playing *their own version* of the first-person video game of life.

- No one knows what anyone else is *truly* going through in their three-dimensional experiences, or what *their* perception of our collective and shared three-dimensional world is.

- People who are both in the exact same experience, at the exact same time, can have radically different perceptions of the 'reality' of that experience.

- Your 'reality' is *subjective* to your specific and personal combination of resistance, (dis)ease, experiences of contrast, energetic or emotional blockages, subconscious programming, and enmeshment with your thoughts, feelings, reactions, and experiences.

- Not one of us knows the expressions of contrast (trauma, abuse, neglect, assault at the extreme end of the negative contrast spectrum) that anyone else has experienced, and it doesn't matter. Because *the weight of any particular contrast* will be felt differently by different people. One person's trauma or potentially deadly three-dimensional experience is another person's peanut butter sandwich. It is all relative to the experiencer.

Who knows what the person that cut you off in traffic might be going through to contribute to their distraction or 'perceived' rudeness? Who can say what the bully who is affecting your child has to survive at home every night?

It is not up to us to judge anyone else's circumstances, experiences, reactions, or behaviors because nothing anyone else does in our three-dimensional world has anything to do with us. Nor does it do us any good to let ourselves be drawn emotionally, reactively, or through thought into resistance to someone else's experience because...

...nothing anyone else does in your three-dimensional experiences has anything to do with the energetic-you! This can be challenging at first, but it isn't a one-and-done thing. This is brain training and expansion practice.

Okay, now let's jump into another thought exercise. Go ahead and grab a piece of paper and pencil again.

The Worst Person in the World: An Exercise in Cognitive Empathy

Think about the 'worst' person you can possibly imagine, dead or alive. Really give yourself a few seconds to think about it. It could be personal (someone you know who you perceive that has wronged you), or a public figure to whom you have resistance. Write the name of whoever you came up with at the top and in the middle of your paper.

It can be anyone but push yourself to consider someone who you perceive as having done 'awful' things, either to you personally or to the world. Remember the more honestly you can challenge your empathetic-self, the more contrast you allow yourself to consider, the more resistance you release, and the more internal growth you will experience on your journey. But go. At. Your. Own. Pace. This is your journey and your journey alone.

Next, create two columns under the person's name you wrote down by drawing a line down the middle of the paper.

On the left side of the line, write down all the bad things that they did. Write down as many as you can think of, or do some online searching if they are or were a 'public figure' (Adolf Hitler, Pol Pot, Osama Bin Laden, Joseph Stalin, heck—maybe even Andrew Jackson).

When you are done with the negatives, it is time to put yourself in that person's shoes. On the right side of the line, write down all the possible circumstances, experiences, thoughts, and influences you can think of that could have contributed to the things that you've written down on the left side of the line. *With cognitive empathy*, challenge yourself to research or come up with as many scenarios, emotions, and thoughts as you can that may have contributed to them doing the things that you wrote down on the left side of your page. Do not stop at 'they were awful people.' That is lazy and an empathetic cop-out.

This is about expanding your capacity for empathy and kindness with yourself, as well as everyone else in your three-dimensional world.

I'll use the Osama Bin Laden example as an illustration:

Osama Bin Laden	
'Horrible' Actions	Radical Empathy
Responsible for US Embassy bombings throughout the late 1990's Responsible for additional terrorist attacks in Egypt, Afghanistan, and Yemen Cultivated, financed, and supported extremist groups throughout North Africa, and the Middle East Directed the hijackers in the attacks on 9/11	According to family he was a good child until being influenced and radicalized by members of the Muslim Brotherhood at University He and the mujahideen that were supported by the USA in Afghanistan fighting the USSR were abandoned after the Soviet-Afghan War in the 1980's [xvi] He felt cultural oppression and that violent jihad was the only option to right what he believed were injustices against Muslims perpetrated by the United States and sometimes by other non-Muslim states. [xvi]

Please note: Radical empathy has nothing to do with justifying 'bad' behaviors, or becoming an apologist for 'bad actors.' This is an exercise in removing the rigidity with which we view our world and realizing that nothing is as black and white as it appears. Whereas a majority of the world probably views Bin Laden as a morally bankrupt and sociopathic terrorist, he very well may have been viewing his three-dimensional world through the lens of being a selfless freedom fighter who had no other option than to attack the western world that once supported him in order to protect his ideologies.

The practice of radical empathy is an exercise in challenging the systems of our three-dimensional constructs and zero-sum perceptions of good and bad, kind and evil, perpetrator and victim, light and dark.

Nothing in life is as black and white as it may be perceived and nothing in life is as clear-cut or easily defined as we may try to make it. But everything in our three-dimensional experiences is subjective to something else. This is where we start moving into the concept of radical balance.

Radical Balance

Radical balance is the concept that everything exists in our three-dimensional experiences exactly as it does because our world, and the systems we have created, of which we are apart and all collectively contribute to, will always strive for balance and require contrast in order to achieve that balance.

Concepts like light and dark, good and evil, birth and death all rely on their counterpart in order for the other side to 'make sense.' How can there be 'light' without the contrasting experience of 'dark' to know what light is? How can we consider something 'good' unless we have a concept of what 'evil' is? Would life be as valuable as it is without an end? They are all necessary.

In order to achieve a sense of radical balance within yourself, you need to accept that there is goodness and kindness in our three-dimensional experiences because we are part of them, and there is bad and evil in our three-dimensional experiences because of our addiction and enmeshment with the feedback we get from the systems we have created, and everything in between is present as well because we live in a radical spectrum of balance. Our three-dimensional world is a perfect balance of contrast for us to observe, experience, and to release resistance. Baby cheetahs are adorable but they need to kill to live, good things happen to bad people, bad things happen to good people, sometimes cheating is rewarded, death is as much a part of life as birth is, life is not fair, and sometimes the good die young.

Does this mean that we just give up and don't take action when we see an injustice, abuse, or assault? No, of course not. But if you approach any of the perceived ills of our three-dimensional world from the *place of the Observer*—without attachment to the negative thoughts, feelings, emotions, and reactions you might otherwise experience in those situations—you will be *much* better equipped in the face of 'perceived' adversity.

Chances are, if you are already expanding your internal fourth-dimensional space, you will be experiencing much less adversity and resistance in your three-dimensional world because you are not operating at the energetic or vibrational end of the spectrum where those energies exist. When you change your vibration, you change the resonance of your life.

Abuser/Abusee Vibrations And Victim/Perpetrator Frequencies

Radical balance is part of radical acceptance and vice versa, but it is also about energetic exchange and connection through vibration and resonance. Both the good and the bad.

In the 'bigger than us' sense, the only reason we are here is to experience the contrasts of our three-dimensional world and release resistance to those contrasts. On the other side of that coin is the concept that everything in our three-dimensional experiences we have either created, co-created, enabled because of resistance, or needed to experience for contrast.

One of the most challenging expressions of the concept of radical balance that I have experienced are the ideas of abuser/abusee vibrations and victim/perpetrator frequencies, and the energetic co-creation of those experiences. This is where we get into the 'deep water' end of the 'radicals' pool.

As I moved through my experiences of expansion and cultivation of quality of body and mind, subconscious mind 'reprogramming', and emotional/energetic release and clearing, I became more and more sensitive to energy.

Other people's energy, my family's energy, ancestral energy, even the energy of places in our three-dimensional world. The energy would manifest as my all-too-familiar personal expressions of (dis)ease: tightness in my chest, shallow breathing, and digestive discomfort.

At first, feeling these symptoms again surprised me because I had been doing my internal work and feeling really good. It was only after doing some troubleshooting and a little digging that I realized the symptoms I was experiencing weren't of my own energy, but of energetic (dis)ease that I was either close to in proximity or connected to ancestrally.

When I started to feel ancestral energy for the first time, it was on a family holiday. Whatever had become stuck in my lineage must have sensed an outlet in my 'openness' to energy because the entire trip, every morning and night, I was clearing ancestral energy that was building up inside me and affecting me physically. It came from multiple generations and many different individuals on both sides of my family line.

Sometimes with energy work, more information, understanding, or awareness is needed before an undesirable condition or emotion can be changed, cleared, or transformed. In the instances of experiencing ancestral energy in which I needed to know more, I was sensorially taken back to 17th and 18th-century Western Ireland, where my family is from. I could smell the 'greenness' of the air, the damp richness of the earth, and the subtle metallic-tang from inside a stone-walled prison. I felt the warmth of a hearth fire and the motionless cool, musty air of an earthen cottage during a family conflict. I felt the crisp, cold edge of a dark night amidst tensions with British soldiers. And, of course, I could feel every one of the emotions that had been stuck in my lineage. From despair and hopelessness, to guilt, horror, sorrow, anxiety, disgust, and rejection.

Because all of this was still so new to me, and at the time I didn't know how to 'turn it off', regulate, or transform it, I was constantly absorbing or being impacted by the energy around me. For weeks I tried to slow or stop the flood of energy by closing myself off to it, but at some level of energetic connection and consciousness, there was a vibration and frequency I was emitting that kept me rooted firmly where I was and enmeshed with the experience.

Consciously, after my wife would help me clear a day's worth of energy that wasn't mine and I was feeling physically better, I would think to myself, *"Well, it's inconvenient and it doesn't feel good, but*

I am helping 'them' (and my entire family) by clearing this energy"
or *"Even though this feels sucky, I don't want to turn my back on
it. What if I turn it off and can't help anyone else?"* There was an
aspect of dysfunctionality or co-dependence to the whole energetic
exchange, but at the time I didn't have tools to experience it any
other way.

Fast forward two years. I had finally cleared all the ancestral
energy that presented itself to be released and, as I continued to
work on myself on my journey of inward expansion, the energy I
would absorb, or allow myself to be affected by, became less severe
and less impactful. I was feeling expansive, lighter, more present,
freer, and more content. Until one summer afternoon. It was a
bigger gathering for the Fourth of July, with a lot of older friends
and acquaintances that I hadn't seen in a long time, as well as a
lot of people that I didn't know. Lots of energy moving around.
After greeting one friend I hadn't seen for years with a hug, we
began talking and they shared how challenging their last few years
had been. An emotionally charged separation; kids having trouble
with sleeping, anxiety, and school; a big move; a job change—all
impactful three-dimensional experiences of contrast.

More people arrived, and we separated to greet other friends,
but I felt those familiar physical symptoms of when I would take
on energy that wasn't mine welling up: the shortness of breath,
tightness in my chest, feeling like I had no internal room to move,
and gastrointestinal discomfort. Since it felt somewhat familiar to
what I had experienced previously, I excused myself from the party
and went out to the car to take care of whatever energy needed to
be cleared.

Once I sat in the car I used muscle testing to discern if this energy was mine, or if I had absorbed it from someone else. It came back strong that it was absorbed from someone else. Going on an intuitive hunch, I checked if it was from my friend with whom I had just spoken. It was. Then I checked if to see if it was *their* energy, or energy from something else, and that was when all hell broke loose.

Whatever energy I had absorbed, attracted, or took on, was dark. It was dark and it felt 'bad.' I was so glad that my friend didn't have this energy anymore, but holy cow, this was like nothing I had ever experienced before and I was *not* ready for it.

As soon as I started to go through my process of cleaning energy, whatever it was started to fight back. It energetically felt like I was being lacerated on the inside by razor-sharp claws and teeth. It felt like I was being shredded from the inside out. My mind went dark, and I started to have all kinds of negative thoughts and feelings toward myself and others erupt into my field. I broke out into a cold sweat and physically began to shake. All of my insides felt like a seething, writhing mass of darkness. I fought through it and would clear a few things, but then more and more would pop up. The experience stretched on for what felt like an eternity, but in retrospect was probably no more than thirty or forty-five minutes. After I finally cleared what I thought were the last remnants of whatever 'it' was, plus whatever other negative energy was present at the time, I was shook. I felt weak and hollowed out, like a husk of myself. I felt hurt, I felt violated, I felt angry, I felt furious, I felt ashamed, I felt deflated, I felt defeated, and I felt used.

Now because of the nature of energy and the role I played in co-creating this energetic exchange, the resonance of this experience and this dark energy lasted. It wasn't until weeks later, only after I diligently worked on myself energetically, that I was finally able to wipe the last remnants of that experience from my energetic and vibrational field.

Unfortunately, I know some of you have experienced similar traumas all too viscerally, all too closely, and much more severely than the example I just shared. Please remember that the contrast we experience in our lives is completely subjective to the experiencer.

No one can tell you anything about your specific experience because no one is you, and no one else has had the extremely personal and unique-to-you combination of life-elements (specific genetic expressions, brain chemistry, thoughts, feelings, emotions, family history, ancestral energy, talents, interests, the life you were born into, the examples, experiences, information, and influences you have moved through in your life) that only you have.

Fully releasing resistance to, and clearing energetic connection or resonance from, negative experiences when you are ready for yourself (and yourself alone) is one of the biggest steps you can take to healing and reducing the impact your past three-dimensional experiences can have on your current and future journey. Seek out an energy healing practitioner, PSYCH-K® facilitator, or Emotion Code Practitioner to help you heal and grow.

Section VI

The Fourth Dimension and Beyond

"Before enlightenment -
chop wood, carry water.

After enlightenment -
chop wood, carry water."

– Zen Buddhist Proverb

By beginning to treat my three-dimensional experiences *dynamically* and *objectively* as the Observer, instead of subjectively as the experiencer, I was able to create the space to begin expanding my internal thought spectrum. That is when I was able to begin incorporating the thought *practices* of radical honesty, acceptance, empathy, and balance into my life, for myself and for others.

But then I met 'My Guy', and what felt like a vast expanse of fourth-dimensional space as the Observer was reduced to the size-equivalent of a pinhead. I feel like I am at the start of an amazing new journey because there is so much more beyond our three-dimensional experiences and Observer perspectives that are waiting for us to be able to connect with.

This is what I feel, and what I know.

Strengthening your intuition, expanding your capacity for compassion for yourself and others, and being able to 'hear' your true inner voice, unencumbered by three-dimensional biases, are just some of the amazing results you will encounter on your journey toward becoming your own Observer.

And, by experiencing those results you will find yourself tapping into the energetic grids that connect all things and fully engaging with your unencumbered spiritual energy. This is where you can cultivate and experience true prosperity.

Your Individual Experience on Your Journey and the Internal Expression of Your Higher Self Will Be Unique to You

We are all at different places in our journeys, moving at different speeds, and at different points in our collective field.

Not everyone that is alive right now wants to, will, or even can look beyond their own three-dimensional experiences and expand into their internal space, and that is perfect. Because they are exactly where they are supposed to be on their own journey and we live in a system of radical balance.

Some of us are already our own Observer, and maybe have been for a long time, but might not ever make their own stronger connection to whatever is just beyond us, and that is perfect too because they are exactly where they are supposed to be on *their* journey as well. Living a fulfilled life of abundance is an amazing journey to be on.

I can't guarantee everyone who reads these words will make their own connection, because I am not you, and you are not me. But I can guarantee if/when you do, it will be an exponentially individual and personal connection with your own expression of what I came to interpret as 'My Guy on the 9th Floor.' You are the only you that could ever exist in this time, in this place, and in this space, and I am so glad that you are on a journey of internal expansion, growth, discovery, and fulfillment that you will be able to share with the world.

Because more so than striving for an end-goal or an end-to-the-journey, please remember the journey is the goal. I've been on an amazing, challenging, frustrating-at-times, emotional, expansive, surprising, and unexpected journey so far, and like I said, I am just getting started.

The more each and every one of us moves into our own internal space as the Observer, and subsequently brings the understanding, empathy, peace, joy, and happiness that is cultivated there out into our overlapping and entangled three-dimensional experiences, the more we are all collectively elevated toward the potential to experience the same. If I am here for me, and you are here for you, then we are all intrinsically here for each other. Because even though this *is* a journey further into yourself, it is *not* a journey of isolation, because we are all energetically connected.

We are just beginning to scratch the surface of what we can do with these badass bio-machines when we're not squabbling over perspectives of subjective three-dimensional experiences.

Engaging with our world from an energetically-connected Observer perspective has the potential to revolutionize the very fabric of our three-dimensional systems, how we treat each other and our planet, and how we look at health, wellness, sickness, and (dis)ease.

The journey into the future begins with each of us taking our own personal journey within. No one else can walk your path.

No one else can take this journey for you, and we can only withstand the (dis)ease in our lives for so long before a 'change' becomes mandatory. All your journey requires is a series of self-reflective, self-aware, positive, empathetic, honest, and balanced choices with an *idea* of the positive outcomes you want to experience. Make one change today, and then make another one tomorrow.

We stand at the precipice of this journey-within alone, but together. The path is laid out in front of us, the messages have been given to us and passed down through the ages, and been built upon, grown, and expanded. This can be the dawning of a new energetically-connected age of humanity.

Continuing to arrive at my own answers to these concepts, as well as moving through the radicals, is the path that I took to just be *ready* to experience how much more there is to our existence than the sum of our three-dimensional perceptions.

Mr. Rogers, obviously, and to no surprise, had it right all along: "Take care of yourself, and each other; and always look for the helpers."

Look for help along the way. Help in many varied, sometimes obvious/sometimes not, and creative ways will find its way to you, and you to it, because everything is connected through energy, vibration, and resonance. Stay open.

If your journey of growth is honest, empathetic, and balanced, you will be massively helping yourself *and everyone else* move further into the role of the Observer, and find greater connection to our energetic-selves.

Keep expanding your ability to experience contrast and release resistance to that contrast. This is how we can unite as a people, and this is how we can save ourselves from ourselves. It's time to get radically honest, empathetic, balanced, and accepting with ourselves, and with everyone else. The unique and perfectly individual 'answer' you are looking for is only found by journeying within.

Live, love, grow, and enjoy the heck out of your journey.

I am so excited for what comes next!

Links & Resources

All resources, links, charts, and workbook exercises
can be found at:

www.myguyonthe9thfloor.com/resources

Endnotes

i.   Various articles around that time included:
        Slawter, Clayton R. (1931, Vol 119, No.4) "New Found Cannibal
        Germs Hailed as Mighty Weapon in War on Disease." Popular Science
        Monthly, p.17
        Jones, Newell. (1938, May 6) "Cancer Blow Seen After 18-year Toil
        by Rife." San Diego Evening Tribune
        Jones, Newell. (1938, May 11) "Rife Bares Startling New
        Conceptions Of Disease Germs And Their Activity." San Diego
        Evening Tribune
        1938, September 23. "Great Interest is Shown in New Rife Ray." San
        Diego Union
        1949, August 4. "Virus Discovered by Laboratory Technician in San
        Diego May Solve Cancer Problem." News Press
        Lynes, Barry. (1986, February) "The Cure for Cancer was Covered
        Up." The Planet Newspaper

ii.   Amit Sharma, Awadhesh Kumar Maurya. *Aggregate Frequencies Of
        Body Organs.* International Journal Of Electrical, Electronics And
        Data Communication. Volume 5, Issue 11, Nov. 2017

iii.   Hawkins, David R. *Power Vs. Force: The Hidden Determinants of
        Human Behavior.* Carlsbad, Calif: Hay House, 2002

iv.   Juan Yin, Yuan Cao, Hai-Lin Yong, et al. *Bounding the speed of 'spooky
        action at a distance'.* Shanghai Branch, National Laboratory for
        Physical Sciences at Microscale, and Department of Modern Physics,
        University of Science and Technology of China, Shanghai 201315,
        China
        Bussières, F., Clausen, C., Tiranov, A. et al. *Quantum teleportation
        from a telecom-wavelength photon to a solid-state quantum memory.*
        Nature Photon 8, 775–778 (2014)

v.   Puthoff, Harold. (1989) *Gravity as a zero-point-fluctuation force.*
        Physical review. A. 39. 2333-2342. https://www.researchgate.net/
        publication/13386630_Gravity_as_a_zero-point-fluctuation_force

vi.   https://www.ribbonfarm.com/2015/08/20/qft/

vii.   https://www.elmergreenfoundation.org/wp-content/
uploads/2018/12/Copper-Wall-Research-Psychology-and-
Psychophysics.pdf

viii.   http://www.worlditc.org/f_08_tiller_subtle_0_energies.htm

ix.   https://www.healthline.com/nutrition/how-much-protein-per-day

x.   https://ourworldindata.org/agricultural-land-by-global-diets

xi.   http://www.fao.org/animal-production/en/

xii.   https://www.health.harvard.edu/staying-healthy/should-you-try-the-
keto-diet
https://www.nutraingredients.com/Article/2019/09/03/Keto-diet-
could-damage-liver-health-say-experts

xiii.   https://news.microsoft.com/ja-jp/2019/10/31/191031-published-
the-results-of-measuring-the-effectiveness-of-our-work-life-choice-
challenge-summer-2019/
https://www.npr.org/2019/11/04/776163853/microsoft-japan-says-
4-day-workweek-boosted-workers-productivity-by-40

xiv.   https://www.theguardian.com/money/2019/feb/19/four-day-week-
trial-study-finds-lower-stress-but-no-cut-in-output
https://4dayweek.com/four-day-week-trial
https://static1.squarespace.com/static/5c3e9f3555b02cbca8b01aab/
t/5c6639880d929730b229a363/1550203293110/Four-Day+Week+
White+Paper+February+2019+final.pdf

xv.   https://www.theguardian.com/world/2018/aug/03/osama-bin-laden-
mother-speaks-out-family-interview

xvi.   https://en.wikipedia.org/wiki/Osama_bin_Laden

Glossary

Bio-machine - the physical 'us'. The collection of our senses, body, physical receptors, and our conscious/subconscious minds

Biofeedback - a process whereby electronic monitoring of a normally automatic bodily function is used to train someone to acquire voluntary control of that function

Conscious Mind - the analytical, problem solving aspect of our bio-machines

Consciousness - the awareness that you are a thinking, feeling being, and is the practice of observing your conscious life (your internal thoughts, feelings, and reactions as well as your external three-dimensional interactions) as you experience it

Dimensions - Different expressions of perceptual reality

3rd Dimension - everything we can perceive with our physical receptors - our senses, our body, our conscious mind, and our subconscious mind

4th Dimension - the conceptual internal space through which we can observe our world and our thoughts, emotions, and reactions without attachment

5th Dimension - a dimension of pure energy that permeates everything we can perceive and that we, as energetic beings, are connected to, part of, can influence, and are influenced by. Oort fields, chakras, collective consciousness, and auras are all part of the energetic connection layer coursing through everything in the universe

6th Dimension - spiritual/God energy. We are all a part of it, it is our energetic core, and it is a part of everything we can perceive with our three-dimensional receptors. This is our origin. Where we come from and to where we all return

(Dis)ease- any negative influence that can manifest physically, spiritually, mentally, or emotionally and cause imbalance and degradation of an energetic system

Emotional Resonance - the energy signature that remains after an emotion is experienced

Energetic Self - The brilliant, beautiful, and perfectly complete 'internal you' that is separate from your 3-dimensional receptors. The connection to your heart, the positive 'voice in your head', and your balanced and empathetic center

Grounding (Earthing) - A therapeutic technique that involves doing activities that physically "ground" or electrically reconnect you to the Earth

Hertz (Hz) - measure of energetic frequency. 1Hz = 1 cycle/second

Hook-up (Whole Brain) Posture - a crossed leg, crossed arm, and clasped hand body posture that activates both hemispheres of the brain. This posture can help return balance, calm, and a stronger connection to your Observer

Muscle Testing - a biofeedback technique that utilizes the body's neurological system as a communication tool to assess what's going on within your body and mind

Non-Locality/Quantum Entanglement - the apparent ability of objects to instantaneously know about each other's state, even when separated by large distances (potentially even billions of light years), almost as if the universe at large instantaneously arranges its particles in anticipation of future events

Observer - the internal perspective of objective observation of our 3-dimensional experiences, our bio-machine's interaction with our 3-dimensional world, and our thoughts, emotions, and reactions

Perceptual Reality - Our individual lens through which we view our world. The collection of 3-dimensional receptors (out bodies, senses, and conscious/subconscious minds) as well as the connection our energetic-selves influences the way we view the world around us

Psychological/Applied Kinesiology - a way of evaluating structural, chemical, and mental areas of health by using manual muscle testing (MMT) along with conventional methods

Quantum Field - a connected grid of energy waves, all potentially in different states of excitation or vibration. The energy waves in a quantum field are the observable particles (matter) in the field

Rife Machine - Biofeedback therapy machine created by Dr. Raymond Royal Rife that purportedly cured cancer in patients under treatment by returning balance to the patients energetic systems

Subconscious Mind/Super Computer of You - the repository of all of our involuntary, bodily/systemic actions (the autonomic nervous system: breathing, heartbeat, digestive functions) as well as our three-dimensional drives, impulses, fears, instincts, emotions, reflexes, and reactive behaviors. Additionally, the subconscious mind is the repository of every single experience you have ever had, even since before you were born

Three-Dimensional Receptors - our physical bodies, senses, and conscious/subconscious minds

Watt - a measure of electrical, energetic output

Whole Brain (Hook-up) Posture - a crossed leg, crossed arm, and clasped hand body posture that activates both hemispheres of the brain, that helps to return balance and calm to an agitated system (fight or flight)

Wim Hof Method - a breathing and physical-stimulation practice that heightens bodily oxygen levels by expelling more carbon dioxide than it lets in

Zero-Point Energy - the lowest possible energy that a quantum mechanical system may have. Even at the temperature of absolute zero, there is still energetic activity

About the Author

Designer and first-time author Kevin Russell is an energetic intuitive who helps people optimize their lives energetically. Professionally for the last 20 years as a UI/UX (User Interface/ User Experience) Designer and Experience Strategist, he specialized in designing creative solutions that guided a user on a journey, through an experience, to an intended outcome.

After a profound encounter of connecting to his higher self, he realized that by coupling the skills he had honed professionally with what he had learned on his own journey of self-discovery, he had the keys to guide others at lightning-fast speed through a step-by-step process to experience the self-awareness, self-expansion, and healing that is so deeply needed today for each of us as individuals, and collectively as stewards of our planet.

WEBSITE **radicalenlightenment.com**

FACEBOOK **@radicalenlightenment**

INSTAGRAM **@myguyonthe9thfloor**

TWITTER **@llessurnivek**